CRAFT AND ART

Fiorella Cottier-Angeli

CERAMICS

 VAN NOSTRAND REINHOLD COMPANY
New York · Cincinnati · Toronto · London · Melbourne

Library of Congress Catalog Card Number: 73-13438
ISBN 0-442-30005-0

Printed in Switzerland

Published in 1974 by Van Nostrand Reinhold Company Inc., 450 West 33rd Street, New York N.Y. 10001 and Van Nostrand Reinhold Company Ltd., 25–28 Buckingham Gate, London SW 1E6LQ.

Van Nostrand Reinhold Company Regional Offices:
New York, Cincinnati, Chicago, Millbrae, Dallas.
Van Nostrand Reinhold Company International Offices:
London, Toronto, Melbourne.

Ceramics workshop in Burma

CONTENTS

*Proto-Corinthian pitcher, second half VIIth century
B.C. Painted terracotta (detail)*

1 INTRODUCTION

Villanovan urn, black impasto, IXth–VIIIth century B.C.

Clay provokes the urge to create.

Men everywhere, from the beginning of time, have squeezed clay in their hands. The history of ceramics is the history of Man. Ceramics illustrates Man's creativeness and his evolution, it records his customs, ideas and religions and reflects his interests. In mastering ceramics Man overcame the fear and fascination of fire; for fire alone gives a mixture of earth and water permanence, hardness—and also brittleness.

The word ceramics comes from the Greek 'Keramos'. It was first introduced to modern languages in 1768 by the archeologist Passeri and applies to all artefacts of fired clay.

In this book the potter's craft will be described by taking in turn the successive stages of work—preparation of the clay, forming, surface treatment, firing—and the techniques corresponding to each rather than by studying finished ceramics.

The best-known types of ceramics are terracotta, pottery, earthenware, faience, stoneware and porcelain.

- Terracotta can be defined as clay modelled and fired but not glazed.
- Pottery is the general name for all vessels made from clay.
- Earthenware vessels are coated with glaze (often lead glaze)–they are usually popular in nature.
- Faience is characterised by its whiteness, obtained either by an opaque enamel over coloured clay, or by a transparent glaze over whitish clay, both of which are fired at variable temperatures.
- Stoneware ceramics are made of opaque clay and fired at a high temperature.
- Porcelain is composed of *kaolin*, feldspar and quartz, after a first firing it is fired at a high temperature, with a glaze or *couverte* of the same components. The qualities of porcelain are its whiteness, translucence, lack of porosity, strength and crystal-like ring.
- Soft-paste porcelains vary in their composition, usually they are based on *glassfrit* and white-clay, which are fired in two firings at temperatures considerably lower than the firing-temperature of real porcelain.

Everybody has his own idea of what constitutes 'real ceramics', settling on one of the following: porcelain, faience, earthenware or stoneware. Ceramics can either be considered as an aspect of archaeology or, alternatively, as a contemporary art-form. It certainly has many facets. It has been practised all over the world throughout history.

Underside of Ming bowl, Kouan. Text incised ulteriorly. Crackled porcelain

9

Firing temperatures

Ceramic

Coloured body

— Porous
- Terracotta for architecture and decoration — 950°–1000°
- Refractory clay — 1300°–1400° and upwards
- Earthenware
- Engobe pottery
- Majolica — 900° to about 1000°
- High-fired faience with unfired enamel

— Impermeable
- Salt-glazed stoneware
- Oriental stoneware
  - Household stoneware — 1100°–1200° / 1200°–1250°
  - Art stoneware — 1200°–1300°

White body

— Porous — Faience
- Soft, high lime content — 900°–1050°
- Hard, high feldspar content — 1200°–1300°

— Impermeable — Porcelain
- Hard
  - Biscuit-ware — 1350°–1400°
  - Household porcelain — 1350°–1380°
- Soft-paste porcelain
  - Glass-frit porcelain — 1150°–1250°
  - Feldspathic porcelain
  - Vitreous China — 1250°–1300°
  - Phosphatic porcelain
  - Bone China — 1200°–1250°

2 CLAY AND ITS PREPARATION

Clay, thanks to its plastic qualities, the ease with which it can be shaped and its permanence after firing, is the basic material of all ceramics. The chemical formula of this more or less pure aluminium silicate is $nAl_2O_3 \cdot nSiO_2 \cdot xH_2O$. The impurities in clay are normally organic humus and various minerals also found in the sedimentary clay-beds and clay mother-rock. Kaolin is the purest form of clay.

Clay varies in colour from whitish grey to a red brown depending on the percentage of impurities.

The clays used for earthenware, faience, stoneware or porcelain all contain the same basic chemical elements, differing only in their relative pureness and their mineral content. The degree of pureness and the combinations of minerals can vary greatly,

and, depending on the firing temperature, can give rise to such a host of different properties and characteristics that it would hardly be possible to include them all within the framework of this book. It is, however, worth mentioning the technique known as *la chamotte*, in which pulverised terracotta is mixed with clay to reduce its plasticity and shrinkage. It is particularly suitable for large-scale work.

The table on page 10 should help the reader. Although simplified, it is generally accurate.

High-fired faience is composed of about 40% pure clay, 35% quartz and 25% feldspar.

Quartz is the most common form of silica. It increases the whiteness of the clay body; as a thinning agent it modifies its composition by altering its plasticity; it also reduces shrinkage after firing while controlling the coefficients of expansion. As for feldspar, it reduces the fusing temperature and thus facilitates the *fluxing* action of the pure clay and silica. Clays suitable for ceramics make up a large part of the earth's crust, they are found in alluvions, either primary beds long since buried under suc-

First stage of refining: the clay is crushed

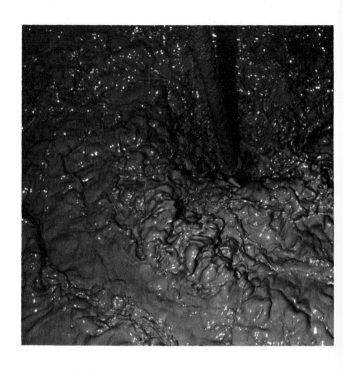

ceeding layers of earth or secondary deposits washed out from the beds of fast-moving torrents.

Extraction techniques vary depending on the place and the level reached by local industry.

Before it can be formed clay must be refined by a series of operations. Dry clay is first crushed, so that it can next be evenly

Soaking and stirring: the clay is given a soup-like consistency

The clay slime is filtered

Second filtering and draining in a cloth-filter press

After filtering the cakes of clay are stored in a damp place

dampened. Once the clay is wet, it is sifted to remove the coarsest impurities (mostly pebbles and organic humus). The slime thus obtained is first soaked and vigorously stirred then filtered and drained in a cloth-filter press. The small, round, plastic, workable cakes of clay obtained from the press are stored in a damp, airtight place. The clay is left to stand for a period which may vary between a few weeks and a couple of decades. It is then cut and *beaten up* in a *pugmill* to prepare it for shaping by eliminating all air-bubbles, which are harmful during forming, to produce the right even consistency and plasticity.

Nowadays these operations are nearly always carried out mechanically, although they are still done by hand in many developing countries.

This preparation of clay, which few people think about, is of capital importance, for the potter's work depends on the qualities of his raw material. Pebbles must be carefully removed: their calcination, when a pot is being fired, would inevitably shatter the clay surrounding them. Uneven consistency causes internal tensions which result in cracked ceramics.

3 FORMING CLAY

There is only a limited number of basic forming techniques, but a skilful potter, armed with the knowledge and know-how gleaned from personal experiments, can combine them in ways that bring about original and often surprising results, such as marbling, *champlevé,* or *slip* relief decorations.

Modelling

This technique is without doubt the most ancient way of forming clay and also the most simple. The plastic qualities of clay allow it to be shaped directly, either with fingers or with a few rudimentary tools—a spatula, scraper or knife. The quality of a piece depends on the modeller's skill. It is the modeller who is responsible for the great diversity of terracottas, some of which are of such perfection that they compare favourably with sculpture.

Large-scale works in bas-relief are usually cut into a number of parts each of which is partially hollowed out so as to dry better, shrink more evenly and be safe from accidents due to expansion. The joints thus

Forming by beating in Afghanistan

Indian beater and block

The work is built up by coiling

created are either regular in shape and therefore apparent, or irregular, in which case they stand out much less.

Works in the round are formed hollow so that they can be dried and fired without breaking or becoming deformed. Small holes or slits are pierced through their walls to prevent them from shattering during firing.

Making the inside and outside uniformly smooth

Vases formed by hand-modelling are shaped either by *beating* or by *coiling*. In the latter method a sausage of clay is coiled round and up, the surface being made uniformly smooth both inside and outside as the pot is built up. By working step by step the potter can ensure constant thickness and density. This most ancient and widespread technique is still used today. In the beating technique, the rough shape of a pot is first made up, then this shape is beaten on the outside by a bat held in one hand, whilst some hard object, usually a stone, is held by the other hand against the inside. This beating enlarges the work and squeezes it upwards.

Throwing
The idea of a potter is always associated with the image of a man working at a throwing-wheel. Throwing is certainly the best known of all ceramic techniques. It illustrates both creativity and the mastering of the basic material. With his hands the potter achieves a delicate balancing act between the soft clay and the form his creative will imparts to it, a form which will become permanent by drying and firing.

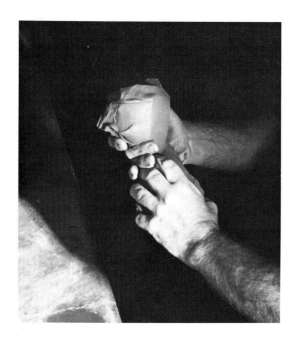

First stage in throwing, a ball of clay is centred on the throwing-head

The best-known throwing-wheel consists of two wheels revolving in a horizontal plane. The lower wheel, spun by the potter's feet, turns the upper wheel–the *throwing-head*–to which it is connected. This type of wheel has been in use throughout history, the only difference now being that electricity has relieved the leg-work.

◁ *Clay is kneaded before throwing*

The potter opens the clay with his thumbs...

◁ *The throwing-head is set in motion by the action of the potters feet on the lower wheel*

...to form the base

The work is squeezed again and the sides of the pot begin to take shape

In some countries a single wheel is used. The potter, crouching, spins it either with his foot or by hand.

To start with, forming on a throwing-wheel is done by hand: a ball of clay is placed on the wheel then centred and raised by being run against the potter's hands.

Next the potter opens the mass of clay with his thumbs to form the base and draws it up towards the final shape by applying pressure through a series of pinches.

A wheel can also be used to pare down the surface of a previously formed green-hard pot. The potter turns the pot over on a

The sides are thinned down by applying pressure to the clay between both hands

The neck begins to take shape...

...then turns out to form the rim

21

stand of the same material, then revolves it against a special scraper to reduce the thickness of the walls; this imparts a characteristically trim and vigorous look to a vase. It is a technique also used for shaping pot feet.

Using a profile or former, the potter can also shape the exterior of a pot the interior of which has been moulded previously.

Only circular forms can be thrown on a wheel. All modifications or attachments such as pouring-lips, spouts and handles are carried out separately. Handles are often formed by *drawing* and fixed to the pot with slip (clay so wet as to resemble a thick soup).

◁ ◁ *Finishing the rim*

◁ *The wheel is halted, lobes are formed by a series of pinches*

The pot is removed from the wheel

A work is turned over on a stand fixed to the wheel

The foot is hollowed out and the sides of the pot are also turned: the pots profile becomes more clean-cut

Archaic Italian pitcher with tin-based enamel and lead glaze, middle XIIIth century

Formers for drawing

Handles, formed separately, are stuck on with slip

26

Turning with a former or profile

27

Clay is cut into even slices and placed over the mould...

...and takes on its shape

Moulding

Moulding is an ancient and well-used technique. It was not only understood by early Mediterranean civilisations but also by pre-Columbian Americans. The latter, not having mastered the wheel (and hence wheel-throwing), developed moulding as their main pottery technique.

Essentially, moulding consists of pressing down clay on and into a negative form of the shape desired. Ancient moulds were generally made of terracotta, nowadays they are more often made of plaster. The original, of which several examples are desired, and which is used for making the mould, is formed, as a rule, by modelling.

The work is removed from the mould

If the mould is relatively flat thin slices of clay are cut with a wire, they are laid over the mould and pressed into it to take its shape.

In the case of a more complex mould the potter applies the clay bit by bit with his fingers, consolidating it as he goes along.

Greek Gorgon in moulded terracotta, late VIth, early Vth century B.C.

29

For simple shapes, a one-valve (one-piece) mould is used. Once the clay has been removed all it needs is a little retouching.

For work in the round, however, a piece-mould (made of several parts which fit together) may be necessary. But it is also possible to mould the various component parts of the work separately and cement them with slip.

Small editions can be produced by this moulding technique, each example of which, however, as it calls for a certain amount of finishing, is also worked by hand. So every unit in a series has its own characteristics.

Slip-casting

Slip-casting is a technique which was developed relatively recently by the pottery industry; it is also used for art ceramics.

It consists of applying a thin deposit of clay in a liquid state (slip), to the inside

The mould is filled...
...then emptied when the reaction has taken place
The mould is opened and the work removed

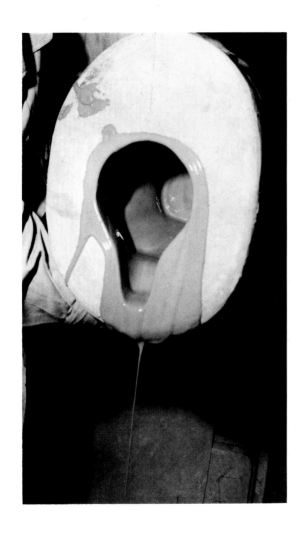

Jean-Claude de Crousaz, box 1970. Enamelled stoneware with engraved decoration

walls of a mould. The mould, which has to be of plaster, is a piece mould.

The slip, once poured into the mould, provokes an electrolytic phenomenon on contact with the plaster; the water is absorbed by the plaster on the surface of which it deposits a coating of clay. This phenomenon is favoured by the addition of soda-based products called deflocculents. It takes from between a minute to half an hour depending on the qualities of the slip. Once the reaction is completed excess slip is poured out. The mould is opened after an hour or two, before the clay dries.

The advantage of this technique is that it produces elaborately worked ceramics with thin bodies of a constant thickness. It is most often used for fine faience ware and for porcelain.

Before moving on to firing, which generally follows forming, something must be said about drying–a most important step in clay work. The aim of drying is to eliminate, before firing, the greatest possible quantity of the water held in the formed clay. If clay is fired while still damp the water it contains vaporizes too violently and the inevitable result is shattered or cracked pots.

During drying the volume of a pot diminishes in proportion to the quantity of water it loses. This diminution of volume is called *shrinkage*. A drying pot shrinks by between 10 and 20%. Kaolin clays dry relatively more rapidly and shrink less than more impure clays.

Goose merchant, *Dresden china, circa 1740*

34

4 SURFACE TREATMENT

It is unusual for formed clay to be left as it is. It generally undergoes several processes which render it impervious to liquids and decorate its surface.

The only exceptions to this rule are pots decorated while still green-hard. These decorations, which are quite common in prehistoric and popular ceramics, are either in 'intaglio', achieved by cords, combing, printing, or with a *roulette,* or else in relief, that is to say built up by *pastillage.*

Surface treatments can be divided into two main categories. In one the surface is treated before the first firing, in the other after a preliminary firing known as a *biscuit firing.*

The possibility of leaving a clay surface as it is, untreated, should be mentioned, however, before discussing the usual treatments; its imperviousness is not guaranteed. In the case of soft-paste porcelain, the effect of leaving a ceramic pot unglazed can be seen in the Sèvres figurines known as 'in the biscuit'.

Geometric Attic Krater. Painted terracotta, second half VIIIth century B.C.

Decorating a surface with a comb

The addition of salt during firing to obtain salt-glazed stoneware can either be considered as surface treatment or as a firing technique.

Burnishing
Burnishing is an ancient technique which makes a clay surface smooth and relatively impervious. It is achieved simply by rubbing the green-hard clay surface. By this method the superficial particles of clay are crushed and the pores between them filled.

Burnishing has also been used as a pre-treatment for glazing—in Greece, for instance. Coloured oxides can be incorporated in burnishing, thus giving it a decorative function; examples of this can be seen in certain pre-Columbian ceramics. Burnished pottery fired in a carbon-saturated reducing atmosphere, acquire a shiny, black, almost metallic-looking surface. Etruscan *buccheri* and Peruvian *chimu* are examples of burnished ceramics.

Engobage and sgraffiato
The techniques mentioned in this section make use of special 'slips'. These differ in colour and texture from the clay from which the ceramic is formed—they are, in fact, usually whitish. When *engobe* is used to decorate a pot with patches of colour it is dabbed on with a brush. A pot can be entirely coated with engobe instead of glaze, to imitate a white clay-body. Engobes are applied in the same way as glazes. In the *sgraffiato* technique, designs are produced in which the clay-body shows through the engobe: the engobe is scratched off with a pointed tool while still green-hard.

The work is coated with a whitish engobe and decorated by sgraffiato

Decorating untreated clay by painting with an oxide

Pots are burnished and engobes applied before firing.

Glazes, enamels and couvertes
Glazes and enamels are generally considered as two of the most characteristic elements of ceramics. They are vitreous substances whose purpose is to make the surface of ceramic clay smooth and impervious to liquids. They are vitrified on the surface of the clay, with which they become intimately fused through the action of heat. For stoneware they can be applied before firing. In the case of 'biscuits' or porcelain, how-

*Firing during the Renaissance.
Engraving after a drawing by
Piccolpasso (fragment)*

ever, they are usually applied after the first firing.

The compositions of glazes vary greatly so it is impossible to classify them precisely. They may, for simplicity's sake, be grouped under the headings: glazes, enamels and couvertes.

— Glazing is the usual surface treatment for faience-ware, earthenware and soft-paste porcelain.

Glazes have a lead or alkaline boric base, their characteristics being that they are transparent, fuse at low temperatures and vitrify at a second firing. They may be tinted.

— *Enamels* are opaque vitrifiable coatings which may be white or coloured by the addition of metal oxides. Their compositions are usually tin-based, but antimony, zirconium and arsenious oxides are also common bases.

— *Couvertes,* used for stoneware and porcelain, are characteristically hard, they vitrify at high temperatures and fuse closely with the clay-body.

The principal components of glazes, enamels and couvertes are: silica, in the form of quartz, boric anhydride, lead, potassium, sodium, calcium, aluminium, magnesium, tin, antimony and zirconium in the form of oxides.

It is difficult to determine the exact role played by each of the oxides constituting a glaze, enamel or couverte. Some (such as lead) lower the fusing point and add gloss, others (calcium) reduce the coefficient of expansion, yet others (like aluminium) prevent devitrification.

Nowadays their preparation consists of the following four stages:

— Choosing the components
— Dosing the components by weight
— Vitrifying the soluble substances: these become insoluble glass on fusing with certain other oxides; various types of furnace are used for this operation: for small quantities they can be equipped with a crucible which has a hole pierced through the base–the substance in fusion drops into a container filled with cold water thus producing a friable glaze suitable for grinding. The temperature of the furnace must be high enough for the various substances to fuse and combine, but not so high that a number of the oxides evaporate. The vitrified substance *(frit)* once

obtained is crushed and ground in water with the residual components to produce a suspension dense enough to give a satisfactory coating. To this effect kaolin or one of the finer clays is sometimes added to the mixture.

Porcelain glazes do not need to be vitrified as they contain no soluble elements.

Glazes, enamels and couvertes must satisfy various requirements if they are to be successful: they must have a homogenous and regular composition, break up in water, remain in suspension, and adhere sufficiently strongly to the clay for a pot to be handled without its glaze or enamel flaking, and, lastly, have a well-established point of fusion so that the firing can be controlled.

Their composition must also be compatible with that of the pot body. For there is often a difference between the temperatures at which a biscuit-fired pot and its glaze begin to expand. If a pot expands more than its glaze it will shrink more slowly and tend to tear the coating which will flake. But if the glaze shrinks considerably faster than the pot its even texture will tend to break and give rise to a crackled effect. Time and moisture can also cause fired clay to expand and glazes to crackle. Glazes also sometimes become devitrified. Research carried out by the pottery industry has gone a long way towards understanding and overcoming these phenomena.

Glazes, enamels and couvertes can either be themselves coloured, or act as a ground for coloured decoration or even be applied over a coloured decoration. A potter can, as he chooses, add pigments to the clay itself or to unfired enamel, or else apply them to a biscuit-fired pot or over glaze.

When colours are applied directly onto the unfired body of stoneware or porcelain they are said to be 'underglazed'. Decoration on biscuit-fired pottery or on top of unfired enamel is vitrified during a second firing or 'grand firing'.

Decoration over glaze, fired enamel or couverte is known as 'overglaze'; it is vitrified during a third or muffle firing.

The pigments used for pottery are obtained from a powder composed of a metallic oxide and ceramic flux, which ensures their adhesion, by techniques resembling the preparation of glazes, enamels and couvertes. The range of colours available is relatively limited.

Porcelain stoneware horseman with ivory glaze, T'ang period (618–907) (detail)

Clear blue is obtained from cobalt oxide, and sometimes from zinc oxide. Other blues come from iron, copper, nickel or vanadium oxides.

Lead antimonate and lead chromate are the principal sources of yellow, which can, however, be obtained at high temperatures from uranium salts.

Bright red is only possible at low temperatures—from selenium, between 900° and 920 °C. Iron oxide gives a rather brownish red. Chromium salts give various tints of red which vary according to the elements with which they are combined. Purple can be obtained from gold.

Chrome oxide gives a green which resists high temperatures. Copper oxide has also been used (since antiquity, in fact) to produce green.

Manganese and nickel oxides give violet. A mixture of manganese, nickel and chrome oxides gives black.

Nickel oxide gives iron-grey.

Intermediary colours may be obtained from combinations of the above.

It is worth noting, however, that there are no constant compositions for colours—every manufacturer perfects his own.

The application of glazes, enamels and couvertes

Glazes, enamels and couvertes can be applied by brush or by immersion, aspersion, insufflation or vaporization. Their 'frits' are nearly always prepared in liquid suspension for easier application. It is possible to sprinkle a powdered coating onto a damp pot through a sieve, but, given the toxic nature of the compounds, it is extremely dangerous to risk inhaling them.

The dipping or immersion technique consists of plunging the pot (which has previously been cleaned and wiped with a damp sponge) into a thoroughly stirred sediment-free suspension. The potter holds the pot with his fingers, or, better still, with special three-pronged pincers which limit the amount of retouching work. The fluidity of the suspension is varied in relation to the type of enamel or glaze required to control the thickness of the coating. Only the thinnest film is necessary for glaze, but for enamels the coating should be as thick as 'glove-leather', as the Renaissance potter Picolpasso put it. He was the author of the first known treatise on majolica. The thickness of the coating depends on the time of

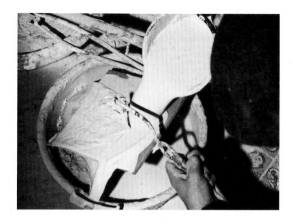

Coating a work with enamel by immersion
The work is removed from the enamel, it is held in
special three-pronged pincers

Coating a work with enamel by aspersion

immersion, the degree of fluidity of the suspension and the porosity of the 'biscuit'. If it is too thin the surface of the pot is irregular; too thick a coating, on the other hand, results in the surface running uncontrollably during firing. The pot is held immersed for a moment or two, then removed and drained in the same gesture to ensure an even coating an immediate drying. This dipping technique is also used for coating unfired clay with engobe. If par-tially vitrified biscuit-fired pots are coated in this manner, organic glue must be added to the suspension to assure its adhesion. The glue burns out during firing.

Aspersion, or pouring, consists simply of pouring the suspension over the pot, with the same result as dipping. Nevertheless, it is more difficult to obtain an even coating in this way. But irregularity may, of course, be the effect that the potter is seeking, if he partially superimposes glazes and enamels,

Decorating over unfired enamel: a tracing brush

for instance. An advantage of pouring is that it uses less suspension.

Coatings can be sprayed on with an insufflator. To avoid sediment the insufflator's reservoir is situated above the nozzle. This method is used specially for applying glaze over unfired enamel decoration and for large-scale work which is too awkward for dipping or pouring, but which calls for a regular surface.

Brush-work is used to obtain special effects of relief and texture, as well as for retouching.

Vaporization is only necessary for salt-glazed stoneware: salt is thrown into the kiln; it vaporizes under the action of heat, saturates the atmosphere and forms a deposit on the pots.

Decoration

The final stage of surface treatment is often the application, over or under the glaze, of decorative elements in colour.

The pottery industry today makes use of several techniques that it has borrowed from other branches of art; these include silk screen printing, printing with rubber stamps and stencilling. There exist, however, certain techniques which belong to pottery exclusively. It is these that are of interest to us here.

Decoration for a second firing is carried out on biscuit, fired engobe or unfired enamel. It is generally coated with an additional film of glaze before being fired— which is why it is said to be 'underglaze'. The potter must always be aware that powdery, flour-like, unfired enamel is extremely delicate and absorbant. His brushwork must be confident and unhesitating, and fairly rapid, because the

The potter avoids touching the enamel with his hands while decorating

moment his brush pauses its liquid load is sponged up by the enamel. The pot must not be touched, so there is a characteristic position for the painting hand. The design is sketched in red lead, the clear red sketch disappears during firing, or else the design is *pounced* on with charcoal powder.

An additional problem crops up with pigments (which, as we have seen above, are limited in number): they bear very little resemblance before firing to the colour obtained by firing. Black may stay black,

but copper oxide green is also black, blue is pale lilac and red mauve.

Two types of brush are used for applying ceramic colours. The first consists of the few hairs which actually draw the fine stroke, surrounded by more, shorter hairs acting as a sort of reservoir for the liquid colour. They enable the potter to trace long lines—this often influences the style of the decoration.

Long linear decorative elements can be obtained by turning the pot on a turntable while the brush is held practically still against it. The second type of brush resembles that used for water-colour painting: it is used for colouring the surface.

The need to hold the brush against the coating without applying pressure and the mental effort involved in predicting the final colours mean that a potter-painter is no ordinary artist, and that an artist cannot, until he has survived many a disappointment, consider himself a ceramic painter.

When unfired enamel, biscuit or engobe have been decorated, a film of glaze is applied to the pot before the second firing (which is often the last).

Some high-fired overglaze colours fuse so

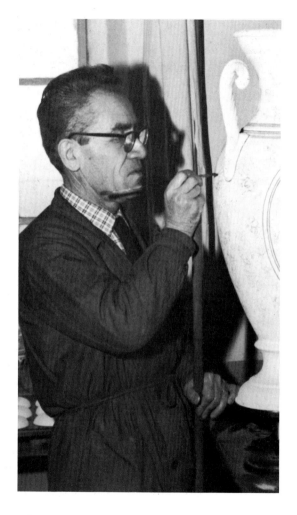

well with their ground of slip or enamel that they cannot be told apart. They start to become incorporated at the moment of fusion, when the substances begin to liquify. These colours and brush-marks acquire a certain vibrant quality.

A third firing is necessary if a greater variety of brighter colours and a design of greater clarity are required. Fewer application problems arise at this stage, but great skill and attention to detail are still necessary. This degree of overglazing is characteristic to porcelain, but it is also suitable for faience, which must have a glossy, vitrified surface. The third firing is carried out at relatively low temperatures and the ground does not fuse again. Only the colour melts, and thanks to the addition of a flux, adheres to the scarcely softened ground. Before colours are applied they are mixed with spirits or resins which act as thinners and adhesives but burn off during firing. Water is unsuitable because the ground is impermeable. The industrial colouring of ceramics makes use of numer-

Pounced decoration. For large-scale work the potter rests his hand on a stick

ous processes from photo-ceramics to transfers, including silk screen printing. But the brush is still the ceramic artist's tool. With it he can demonstrate his skill. He can work with a wide range of colours, using effects such as 'white relief' or playing with the many reds: ruby, purple, coral, shrimp pink.

Gilding and silvering

The same technique is used for both gilding and silvering, but it is, in fact, platinum that is used for silvering—as silver tends to tarnish, and gold is obtained from a mixture of gold salts and a flux. These solutions are applied like other colours. A coating of gold is obtained at low temperatures. It is then shined up using agate or graphite burnishers. This method produces the most satisfactory and permanent gilding. There are other processes which give matt or gloss gilding without burnishing. But the quantity of gold is smaller and the coating less reliable.

Some special decorative effects are obtained during a third firing. They will be described under 'Firing'.

Glaze being sprayed on with an insufflator

47

5 FIRING

The importance of firing is capital, for it is only during firing that the physico-chemical reactions through which the basic raw manufactured objects acquire the specific characteristics of ceramics take place: clay loses its crumbly, shapeable qualities and can no longer be mixed with water, instead it becomes hard and strong, and will never recover its former plasticity; coatings vitrify and fuse with clay rendering it impermeable.

Depending on the compositions of the clay and glazes the chemical changes take place at specific temperatures and under particular conditions. Thus some reactions

Open-air firing in Guatemala

will only take place in an oxidizing atmosphere, others in a reducing atmosphere. They occur at precise moments during firing.

For successful firing it is important to reach the right temperature at the right moment, to be able to vary the atmosphere between oxidizing, neutral and reducing when necessary and to achieve an even heat so that, at any given time, the temperature is constant in every part of the kiln.

Kilns
Firing is done in kilns, the shapes, possibilities and fuels of which vary considerably.

The most primitive kind is simply an open fire: the pots are placed in a hole in the ground and surrounded with fuel—it could be wood, straw or even dung. Traditional pottery is still fired this way in some unindustrialised countries. The potter's means are severely limited as he can only reach a feeble temperature, which he can scarcely control. A lot of material is wasted through breakage and pots fired in this manner are inevitably irregularly smoked.

Since earliest antiquity, however, masonry kilns have been built, in which the

Works held by the finger-tips are placed on tripods

consist of a series of intercommunicating chambers, connected together along an uphill gradient, through which the heat travels, from the combustion chamber to the chimney. The pots are enclosed in *saggars*. Pine wood is used as fuel–its cinders form an integral part of the enamels.

Different types of casettes or saggars after Piccolpasso

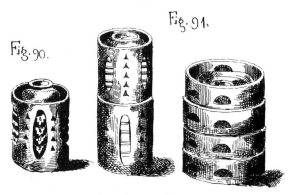

pot chamber is separated from the combustion chamber in order to conserve and control heat. The most common type of kiln consists of a pot chamber situated above a combustion chamber. The chimney can either adjoin this chamber or crown it. The smoke flue is sometimes isolated from the pot chamber.

Chinese and Japanese potters used and still use 'bank-kilns' (Nobori-Gama). They

The forms and basic principles of kilns have changed with the development of the pottery industry—as has the choice of fuel. For art ceramics today, the most common fuels, which have replaced the traditional wood, are oil, gas and electricity.

Packing the kiln
The way in which the kiln is packed is important because of certain phenomena which occur during firing: vitrification only takes place when glazes, slips or enamels fuse; during fusion the pot's coating melts slightly; on cooling subsequent vitrification may cause it to adhere to the material by which it is supported. Also various substances are given off during fusion which can affect neighbouring works. Obviously, then, pots must be arranged and packed up most carefully inside the kiln. They must neither touch each other nor their stands— at least no more than strictly necessary. The temperature throughout the kiln must be as even as possible and the load equally distributed. To this effect objects made of refractory clay are used, including triangu-

Kiln scaffolding

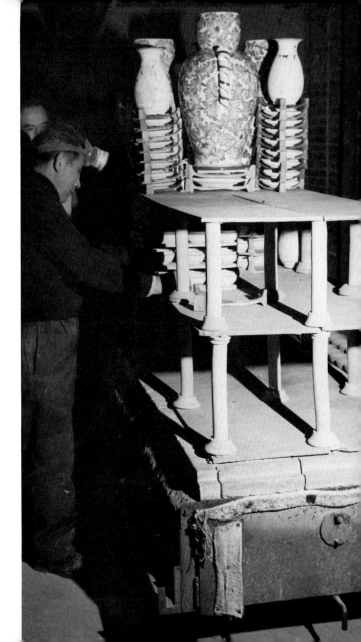

lar chocks, bricks and tripods, also slabs, columns and pillars and special stands equipped with rungs or shelves.

Porcelain and pots with lustre, metallic or other coatings which need to be protected from the gases given off during firing, are placed in saggars (boxes of refractory material already known by the Greeks and Chinese).

No particular precautions need be taken for untreated clay pottery. The pots can even be packed one on top of the other, as long as the weight is evenly distributed to prevent them from becoming deformed.

During firing a number of physico-chemical phenomena occur: remaining water is eliminated, organic matter is destroyed, limestone is calcinized, and the clay body alters as its components are chemically decomposed, changing in structure until it becomes like stone. Throughout this process the volume of a pot varies in a complex fashion as a result of a combination of shrinkage caused by the elimination of remaining water, expansion due to heat and a change in density at the moment

Popular pots piled on top of each other (biscuit-fired work and pots needing a second firing)

of vitrification. These different transformations take place at precise temperatures and at specific stages of firing. At first the kiln must be heated slowly as the fiercest expansion occurs at the beginning of firing.

The maximum firing temperatures depend on the type of ceramic:

earthenware, terracotta	900°– 980 °C
faience	920°– 950 °C
art stoneware	1200°–1300 °C
white faience	900°–1050 °C
soft-paste porcelain	1150°–1250 °C
hard-paste porcelain	1350°–1400 °C

The fusion point of pure clay is 1780 °C. Cooling is also part of the firing process and must be as strictly controlled as heating the kiln.

Controlling the firing

Several processes are used to control firing. The oldest is the potter's eye. The temperature is estimated by colour, so the potter applies his eye to a hole pierced for that purpose in the kiln wall. The kiln materials and atmosphere radiate luminous colour under the effect of heat.

Kiln load ready for firing

The wood-fired kiln is fed with faggots

The colour graduation is approximately the following:

faint red	525°– 550 °C
dark red	650°– 700 °C
bright red	800°– 850 °C
light red	900°– 950 °C
dark orange	1000°–1050 °C
bright orange	1100°–1150 °C
faint white	1200°–1250 °C
bright white	1300°–1350 °C

Eye control is often supplemented by a system of ceramic rings of composition similar to the pots being fired which are lined up close to the control hole and removed one by one with a metal rod during the course of firing.

Silicate cones have also been designed to help potters gauge kiln temperatures. Under the effect of heat, these cones soften at pre-established temperatures. In Europe the Segers system is used; it is graduated in 59 steps from 600 to 2000 °C. The temperature is indicated at the moment the cone's point softens and touches the ground.

The most accurate instrument to have been perfected is the pyrometer; designed to measure high temperatures precisely, it gives the potter minute by minute information on the kiln temperature.

Firing atmosphere

The kiln atmosphere is usually oxidising, which means that it contains more oxygen than the fire needs to burn. An oxidising atmosphere is essential for successful high-fired enamels. On the other hand, certain other compounds and effects can only be obtained if a reducing atmosphere (deprived of oxygen) is produced at various times during firing. Here are a few examples:

– Porcelain is first fired in an oxidising atmosphere, then in a reducing atmosphere to lighten the colours of the ferrous compounds. The final stages of firing and cooling take place in an atmosphere which is once again oxidising.

– Stoneware is fired in an atmosphere which can be either oxidising or reducing, depending on the colours the potter wants. Stoneware colours range between yellow, brown and grey.

– The reducing atmosphere necessary for some types of black pottery is obtained

Flames spurt from all openings in the kiln as the wood begins to blaze

55

Fired work being removed from the kiln

by adding powerful smoke-producing substances during firing which saturate the atmosphere and fill the pores of the iron clay with carbon, rendering it more or less impervious. Etruscan *buccheri* and pre-Columbian Peruvian *chimu* are products of this process.

The rich possibilities of firing in a reducing atmosphere can best be seen in the *lustres* and metallic highlights obtained when a previously enamelled and fired pot is given an additional firing at a relatively low temperature. For faience and majolica this third firing takes place at about 700 or 750 °C. By provoking, with a reducing atmosphere, reactions between the salts of copper, silver and bismuth, amongst others, the potter obtains particles of metal of varying thickness and density. These either cause optical effects by refraction, or form a continuous metal skin. Copper salts give a ruby red, silver salts the iridescent yellow known as *cantharides* lustre, bismuth salts a pearly lustre. These effects are enhanced when obtained over coloured enamels. Metallisation is induced by introducing smoke-producing substances to the kiln to reduce the atmosphere just as the glazes begin to fuse without being able to absorb carbon. Firing is done in a two-storeyed muffle-chamber, often made from sheet-metal. The upper storey contains the pots to be lustred, the lower storey the smoke-producing substances, which can have varied origins: animal horns, hair, sugar, naphthaline or pine resin, will all do.

Industrial research has probed pretty deeply into the complex phenomena which take place during the creation of ceramics and particularly during firing.

But a potter practising the art of ceramics is neither physicist nor chemist. His knowledge of the possibilities of clay is empirical. He learns to imagine how a pot will turn out, but also to accept something different and reap a rich harvest from experience gained in this way.

As the potter William Lee said at the beginning of this century: 'All we ask from a fire is a result somewhere near our predictions.'

Etruscan 'bucchero-style' Oinochoe, circa VIth century B.C.

57

6 FROM THE ORIGINS TO CLASSICAL ANTIQUITY

Origins

It would be outside the scope of this book to write the history of ceramics from an aesthetic, archaeological or sociological point of view.

The filiation, evolution and even dates of many ceramics and the influences they have undergone are still being argued by archaeological specialists. The following summary is based on a selection of important and outstanding pottery, seen in relation to the techniques and traditions which produced it. For questions of dating we have referred to recent publications.

Although the earliest *potsherds* are sometimes attributed to populations of the upper paleolithic age, ceramics did not become an everyday reality until the neolithic period. Pottery made its appearance at the same time as cereal agriculture and domesticated animals. The technique was used to make objects for domestic purposes, usually containers, which have since been found in tombs where they were buried to accompany the dead. It is evidence of a state of civilization. Examples of pottery forms and techniques known to be a good many thousands of years old have been found in Spain, the Scandinavian countries and by the Danube. The coarse, unpurified clay body, called *impasto* is modelled, often by coiling, but also by beating or by using a scraper. It is sometimes burnished. These potsherds are heavy, indicating an open firing at low temperature. Decorative elements have often been added by sgraffiato, printing or cord-decoration methods. Chalice and bell-shaped pots turn up so frequently that this period has been called the caliciform or campaniform culture. Neolithic pottery, with its straightforward forms, is extraordinarily vigorous despite the coarseness of its materials and the scarcity of the means available.

The Near East

The Near East is one of the cradles of civilization. All the peoples living between the Tigris and the Euphrates, in Upper Syria

Winged bull, *Achaemenian, moulded bricks with polychrome glaze, VIth–IVth centuries B.C.*

59

and on the Persian and Anatolian plateaux had master-potters working for them since the depths of time. Pottery dating from the sixth millennium has been discovered in Azerbaijan and Elam. Potters were already using the wheel at Erech, in Sumer, in the middle of the fourth millennium. A kiln has been found at Baku, in Persia, also dating from the fourth millennium, in which the pot chamber is separated from the combustion chamber. Towards the year 3000 B.C. matt pottery starts to be coloured with minerals and slips. Vitrified glazes were invented during the second millennium. Pottery was used for making not only containers of all shapes and sizes, but also ritual figurines, writing tablets, objects of apparel and, above all, decorative mural panels which were integrated with the architecture — the grandeur of which had already impressed neighbouring peoples.

The first pottery wall-coverings, which were discovered at Erech, in Sumer, date from about the year 3000 B.C. They consist of a sort of mosaic of painted clay tacks with petal shaped heads and harpoon-like points which are buried in the wall. At Susa, during the 12th century B.C., potters constructed large-scale mural panels in enamelled ceramics, which probably had a tin-based glaze. In the palace of Sargon II (722–705 B.C.), at Khorsabad in Assyria, near ancient Nineveh, archaeologists found a large panel of flat bricks enamelled in yellow against a turquoise blue background. It is decorated with a frieze of figures representing lions, bulls, eagles and life-sized men. The blue backround was perhaps obtained from lapis-lazuli.

Nebuchadnezzar's palace, in Babylon, contains the god Marduk's Procession Way which ends at the double gate of the goddess Ishtar leading to the throne-room. This was entirely lined with enamelled relief decoration depicting lions, dragons and bulls. The Procession Way itself was more than a hundred metres long and about twenty-four metres high. The colours employed are white, yellow, green, turquoise blue (obtained from copper) and black to draw the figures. The interior of the main walls was formed from bricks bearing the king's name, the exterior from bonded bricks which were pointed with bitumen so as to make the joints less visible. Each brick was numbered and had its appointed place. The relief work was obtained by moulding.

These decorative bricks have obviously been fired twice, first a biscuit firing, then for the enamel.

A great many ceramic panels were made for the palaces of the Persian kings at Susa, in particular for Darius I and Artaxerxes (VI–Vth century B.C.). These friezes, of which only parts are, strictly speaking, 'ceramics', are composed of archers and animals in relief; the material from which they are made contains very little kaolin but is rich in silica, quartz and lime. Other parts are made from clay mixed with unburnt vegetable matter which is a sign that they have not been fired. The pointing of these ceramic bricks was done in lime in such a way as to be clearly visible. A particularity can be observed in the enamelling technique: the colours are separated from each other by slivers of clay to prevent running during firing. The background colour is turquoise blue, the figures are in slate-blue, light yellow, orange and white.

Susa goblet, 4000 B.C. Painted terracotta

It must be one of these panels that is described by the prophet Ezekiel in the Old Testament: '.... she saw men portrayed upon the wall, the images of the Chaldeans portrayed with vermilion, girded with girdles upon their loins, exceeding in dyed attire upon their heads, all of them princes to look to, after the manner of the Babylonians of Chaldea, the land of their nativity.'

Egypt
The main particularity of Egyptian ceramics is the use of glazes and enamels of a characteristic shade of blue which makes it look extremely precious. Much Egyptian work is very small. It is sometimes difficult to tell if it is ceramic or glass-ware, as in the case of the figurines called *ushebti*, which have been found in large numbers in XIVth to IVth century B.C. tombs and are made from an amalgam of clay and enamel. This pottery in fact contains hardly any clay but is siliciferous. It was so difficult to model that before being formed it was probably mixed with resin or organic size which would burn out during firing. On the other

Snake goddess, *siliceous clay with polychrome glaze, Crete, XVIth century B.C.*

hand it was an excellent ground for enamel. The traditional blue was obtained from a frit composed of quartz sand, copper and an alcaline flux. Its nuances depended on the purity of the copper and its combination with ferruginous substances. By the Eighteenth Dynasty potters had a range of twenty colours or more at their disposal. They obtained white from tin and with it gave body to their colours which otherwise tended to be relatively transparent. Blue enamel can already be observed during the fourth millennium, on parts of necklaces. Most Egyptian ceramics, whether moulded figurines or wheel-thrown bowls and cups, were of small dimensions, rarely exceeding 8 inches (20 cm.).

The techniques acquired by Egyptian potters continued to be practised without noticeable change from the Ninth Dynasty (2200 B.C.) up to the Arabian conquest (VIIth century A.D.). Glazed ceramics were also used for interior walls and floors. The oldest known ceramic mural decoration is dated between 2700 and 2800 B.C. It is in the tomb of the pharaoh Zoser, under the

Cretan amphora with a decoration of octopuses, XVth century B.C. Painted terracotta

mastaba pyramid at Sakkara. Ceramic plaques alternate with slabs of white limestone. They represent plaited reeds.

Crete and the Aegean

Between 3000 and 1000 B.C., the seafaring peoples, called *Kefti* by the Egyptians (they were in fact the inhabitants of the Aegean islands and mainland coasts), formed a great civilisation based on their dominion of the sea.

Thanks to the extent of their trade, works of Cretan origin, including Kamares vases, have been found as far off as Upper Egypt, and a considerable number of Egyptian artefacts has been discovered in Crete. Crete was the centre of this civilisation for several centuries, before Mycenae and Tiryns. Ceramics form an important part of its production. Many works merit particular attention: the jars with incised and modelled relief decoration which is so well adapted to their exceptional size; the *rhytons,* those ritual vases shaped like animals—the body or head of a bull, for instance—and the thrown *stirrup-vases* with their vertical handles and out-of-centre spouts. Kamares pottery, called after the

site where it was first discovered, was made around 2000 B.C. It is distinguished by the fineness of the thrown body and by an undulating polychrome decoration of light toned engobes (white, yellow and red) on a bluish-black background; it is frequently based on circles and spirals and most often inspired by marine animals or floral motifs.

The famous 'naturalist' ceramics, which are dated at around the middle of the second millennium B.C., are characterised by dark decorations representing octopuses, squids, coral and other marine life, painted over a light ground. The whole pot-surface is covered by the composition which is executed with great freedom. Finally, the well-known statuettes of goddesses or priestesses holding snakes are from the XVIth century B.C. They are glazed with what is probably an enamel. The colours used are white tinted with ochre or lilac, brown, blackish brown, manganese violet, turquoise blue and green. The clay body has a silica base and resembles that employed by the Egyptians. The glazing technique, unique in the Aegean world, was used exclusively for these idols, which never exceeded 14 inches (35 cm.) in height.

7   CLASSICAL ANTIQUITY

Greece

It is difficult to study Greek ceramics in an unbiased manner, because the student has usually been conditioned by a teaching tradition and culture which are essentially literary in character. Vases are commonly considered merely as 'beautiful' backgrounds for representations of mythological characters. Regret at the disappearance of the *great* mural painting can be felt behind the student's admiration for these smaller manifestations of Hellenic art.

During the period from the Xth to the VIIIth century B.C., the geometric style was developed, principally in Attic workshops; it replaced the protogeometric style (XIth to IXth century B.C.). Geometric potters created vases of various types: amphora, *krater, pyxis,* skyphos. The most remarkable of all are the funerary amphorae, sometimes more than five foot high. Amphorae have been found in large numbers in the Dipylon necropolis at Athens. Their decoration is geometric and relies on elements like waves, herring-bone patterns, chequered effects, lines, swastikas, circles and stylized figures of men and animals, arranged in friezes or metopes. The design is in black; it stands out against the rosy colour of the fired clay ground. It would not be fair to think of these vases as mere steps in the evolution towards human figuration. They definitely have an austere elegance of their own. The figures and geometric motifs are arranged according to strict rules of proportion which give the works coherence as well as a severe harmony.

During the VIII and VIIth centuries B.C., ceramics in an 'Orientalised' style begin to appear; they have been found in many towns and islands. Corinth can be considered the cradle of this stylistic era. Each workshop of course had its own peculiarities, but all pottery in this style had one thing in common: a decoration consisting of zoomorphic friezes, representing real or fabulous animals and plant motifs. The design is engraved in the clay. The colours are red, black and purplish-blue with white highlights. They are applied directly to the terracotta ground. Human figures became part of the decoration of Corinthian vases during the VIth century B.C.

Athenian workshops were at the height of their fame during the VIth and Vth centuries B.C. The painter who decorated a vase was not always the potter, but we know the names of both, for they signed their works. Klitias, the painter, worked with Ergotimos, the potter. Exekias, Psiax and Lysippides painted black figures on a red ground. Epiktetos, Phintias, Euthymides, Euphronius, Kleophadres and Hermonax's signatures are found on works decorated with red figures against a black ground. Their favourite subjects were Homeric heroes, Dionysiac scenes and the great divinities. The representations of well-known characters are often accompanied by their names for easier identification. This was the case for a while for portraits of famous ephebes.

Black figures on a red ground are achieved simply by painting the figures directly onto the previously smoothed and burnished clay vase surface. The design is sometimes heightened by a light sgraffiato. White and violet highlights are also used to accentuate certain parts. Thus female curves are heightened with white.

This type of decoration allowed the painter to demonstrate his skill. The quality of such ceramics certainly depended as much upon the painter's skill as on the potter's throwing and firing techniques. The clay from which these vases are made is compact, a sure sign that it was well prepared. The vase walls are thin—proof that the potters had mastered the art of throwing. The 'tightness' of the forms betrays the use of turning tools. As for the black glaze, with its bluish or silver highlights, its appearance is truly astonishing. Despite its brilliance it is not, in fact, vitrified. It is thought to have been obtained by a one-firing technique. Although the term 'glaze' is commonly used when referring to the surface treatment of these vases, it is inaccurate. Actually, it was a colloidal solution of an engobe made from the same clay as the vase applied to the partially dried, burnished clay body. The different colours

Greek cup with black figures painted by Exekias, circa 535 B.C.

must have been obtained by alternating the kiln atmosphere during firing from, first, oxidising to reducing, then back to oxidising in such a way as to cause variations in the iron oxide contained in the clay. During the first oxidising phase the whole surface becomes red. During the reducing phase it all becomes black and the colloidal engobe adheres to and fuses with the vase surface. When the atmosphere is altered to oxidising again, only the unslipped clay becomes red, at a temperature of 950 °C. At a higher temperature the engobe decoration would also become red. The perfection of this method, for which the kiln atmosphere must be alternated at precise temperatures, is ample evidence of the technical mastery of the Greek potter.

The white-ground *lekythos* vases, made in the Vth century B.C., are equally remarkable. Figures, shown in funeral scenes or in aspects of daily life, were freely drawn in brown or red brushwork on a ground of whitish engobe. The design was heightened with dabs of various tints of colour; yellow, sky blue, green, purplish-blue, red. Funerary lekythos are made up of two parts: the visible decorated vase and a much

Attic lekythos with white ground, circa 440 B.C. (Fragment and view of interior)

Charon pushing his boat, *Attic lekythos with white ground. Vth century B.C.*

68

smaller, hidden container luted to the inside of the top of the vase neck. This arrangement made it possible for the lekythos to contain oils and essences which would otherwise have stained the porous engobe.

Starting during the Vth century and particularly from the IVth century B.C. onwards the techniques developed in Athenian workshops spread all over Magna Graecia and particularly in Apulia. But the shapes, designs and subject matter (whether scenes of an after-life, satirical scenes or theatrical scenes) varied from one region to the next.

Etruria
The Etruscans emerged in central Italy in the VIIIth century B.C. They succeeded the Villanovans, whose cinerary urns are of interest to us. These urns are either shaped like miniature cabins complete with roof and apertures or else biconical with a handle. They were formed by hand; the surface was burnished. Decorative motifs were added by combing, cord-decoration or printing. They were fired in a reducing atmosphere in kilns or in open fires in which they are quite likely to have been piled up together with other vases and the fuel. Their colour varies, but they are usually darker than neolithic vases. The lids of the biconical urns were either reversed cups made of clay or bronze helmets.

The Etruscans, who were united in a federation of twelve towns including Cerveteri, Chiusi, Perugia, Tarquinia and Vulci had a common religion in which the natural elements—earth, water, lightning—divination and the after-life played a major part. They were masters of the terracotta technique and great ceramic-lovers. Their case is exceptional because not only did they produce pottery which reflects their own tastes but they also collected and conserved a good many examples of Greek ceramics. It is, in fact, in large measure thanks to the Etruscans that we know of Greek pottery. They used Greek techniques and motifs, which, however, they adapted to suit their own vision in a way that suggests admiration rather than imitation.

Decorative elements such as *acroteria, antefix,* friezes, low-reliefs, high-reliefs and

Etruscan archaic sarcophagus, VIth century B.C. Polychrome terracotta

statues have been retrieved from destroyed temples. Urns, *canopic vases,* sarcophagi and other funerary containers have been discovered in necropolises, along with a large number of vases in different styles, including the *bucchero* which is of particular interest to us.

The sarcophagi are admirable because of the mastery of firing illustrated by such large-scale work, the able modelling and the taste for individual likenesses in the portraiture. Moulding was used for making acroteria, antefix and friezes in order to obtain a decoration with repetitive motifs.

Buccheri are pots with a uniformly black burnished surface, which the Etruscans produced in different styles throughout their history. The term *bucchero* was coined at the time of the first finds, towards 1700 A.D.; it is a misrendering of the Spanish word *bucaro* which was the name given either to Portuguese copies of odoriferous-bodied vases from Equatorial America or to stoneware imported from China. Buccheri are made out of the ferruginous clay common in Etruria. They were thrown with very clear-cut profiles, burnished with great care while drying and finally fired in a two-chambered kiln in an atmosphere reduced by fumigation. Surfaces obtained this way have a satiny appearance caused by the combination of black given by carbon and black given by the ferrous oxide produced during firing. The oldest style, from the VIIth century B.C., is called *bucchero sottile* because of the fineness of the throwing. It is decorated with incised lines which are sometimes filled with white colouring matter. The decorative motifs of Orientalised buccheri are mainly zoomorphic, carried out by impression with a *rondelle.* During the Vth century B.C., a *bucchero pesante* of large dimensions was manufactured almost exclusively in the Chiusi region. Its thick sides were decorated by moulding and impression. The production of buccheri died out with the disappearance of Etruria as a political entity, at the end of the IVth century B.C.

Rome
The Romans did not intend their ceramics to have artistic value, but in the early ages they gave it the moral value of austerity.

During the Empire terracotta was the basic material for building. With their accumulated wealth, the Romans preferred gold and silver table-ware to pottery, which was restricted to the kitchen.

Apart from the plaques called *Campana* after the founder of the first collection, two types of Roman ceramics deserve our attention:

Aretina ceramics from Aretium (Arezzo), where they were first produced, were copied all over the Empire. They inspired innumerable workshops, the most important being in Gaul, up to the IVth century A.D. The forms were moulded or thrown then printed and coated, after a first firing, with an even coral-red alkaline boric glaze. Terracotta moulds were most often used. This pottery was usually signed with a seal. So it is also known as *sigillated earth*.

Lead-glazed pottery was also common and as widely spread. The glaze, which made the pots impervious to liquids, was coloured yellow, purplish-blue or, more often, green, by the addition of iron, manganese or copper oxides. With the passage of time some of these works have acquired a silvered look caused by devitrification of the glaze. The same lead glazes are being used by potters today.

Gladiator, *IInd–IIIrd century A.D. Fragment of red-glazed Roman pottery with decoration in slip*

8   THE ISLAMIC WORLD

By Islamic ceramics we mean works produced between the VIIIth and XVIIIth centuries A.D. in Moslem countries or in those parts of the world occupied by the Arabs: Persia, Mesopotamia, Asia Minor, North Africa and Spain.

They vary greatly in style but are all characterised by a certain preciosity which is the result of a lively play of colours, enhanced by glazing, by lustres and fantastic decoration. The predilection of the Moslem world for Arabesque can perhaps be explained by the religious idea which is proper to Islam, of the instability of form and body. Representations of human

Aiguière plate, XIth century, Islamic, glaze over engobe

figures are rare, except in Persia, as they were forbidden by the Koran. Because of the difficulties of dating Islamic pottery, archaeologists have had to classify it according to where it was found and the techniques employed.

At Rhages in Persia, Samarra on the Tigris, Rakka on the Euphrates, and Fostat (old Cairo) in Egypt, ceramics dating from the VIIIth to the XIIth centuries have been found—they represent the archaic period. Some have a decoration in brown, yellow and green engraved in engobe under a glaze. The design of others is painted over a stanniferous enamel, often with a ruby-red lustre or one varying from golden yellow to olive-green.

Persia

Persia has always been a leading centre of ceramic art. The *Minai* style of decoration is typically Persian. The presence in it of human figures and the exquisiteness of the design relate it to miniature painting. Works in this style are thought to have been produced in the XIIth and XIIIth centuries at Rhages, Kashan and Sava. The taste of Persian potters for precious work and their technical mastery are exemplified by the use of gold-leaf gilding to heighten ceramic decorations and also, from the XIIIth century onwards, by opalescent effects achieved by filling openings in biscuit-fired pots with the enamel used for coating. These effects resemble the Chinese porcelain *rice-grain* technique; Chinese porcelain had a great influence on Persian ceramics during the XIIth and XIIIth centuries.

Asia Minor

Ceramics made between the XVth and XVIIth centuries in Syria, Turkey and Anatolia, coming perhaps from Damascus, Constantinople and Kutahya are grouped together under the name Isnik (formerly Nicaea, in Asia Minor). Tiles, plates, vases with handles, ewers and mosque lamps were decorated with arabesques and floral motifs: carnations, tulips and peonies. These were first drawn in blue on a white enamel ground or blocked out in white against a blue ground, then later became multi-coloured with the addition of a characteristic but unusual tomato-red. The enamel is extremely white and brilliant. Colours frequently stand out in relief.

Spain

During and after the Moorish occupation Spain also was a great producer of ceramics. Malaga from the XIIIth, Valencia and Manises during the XIVth and XVth centuries were famous centres of the art. Their lustred pottery became very fashionable and was exported, especially to Italy. One of the best-known Spanish works is called the *Alhambra vase;* made at Malaga in the XIVth century, it is more than three feet high, decorated with gold lustre on a white ground heightened with blue representing arabesques, animals and ornamental inscriptions. The decorative themes on pottery from Paterna are more often popular, which suggests a comparison with archaic Italian ceramics. The design is sketched in manganese; it is coloured green or sometimes blue over a tin-based white enamel. Manises pottery is coloured blue with a golden lustre on stanniferous cream-coloured enamel. Armorial plates are favourite themes with epigraphic decoration in Arab or Gothic characters and stylized

Lustred Persian cup, circa XIVth century. Probably from Sultanabad

76

Cup with lead enamel from Paterna, Spain. XIVth century

gazelles, greyhounds or other animals. The main motif is usually depicted in blue over a lustred ground. In the XVIth century we frequently find ruby-red lustre over a yellowish ground. The abundance of lustred works, obtained by metallizing salts of copper or silver during a third firing, is, once again, proof of a perfect mastery of the techniques of firing.

Civilisations influenced by Islam had, as another characteristic in common, a love of ceramics integrated with architecture. In Persia many monuments, palaces and mosques were faced with ceramics. Ceramic plaques served to tile floors, from the XIIIth century onwards in Spain. They were imprinted or made by the process known as *cuerda seca* which gives great clarity of design by preventing the enamels from fusing together. It seems that this consisted in first sketching the design with a brush dipped in grease or wax. The workshops that manufactured floor tiling also produced the *azulejos*—square glazed wall-base tiles.

The sources of inspiration of Islamic ceramics can never be traced by archaeology or history. Despite the fact that they are very varied, they leave us with an overall impression of reverie and visual pleasure. It may be surprising that such an art should have flourished in so harsh and cruel a world, but we must not forget that the features of an Islamic warrior mask that great dreamer: Oriental Man.

Moulded plaque with decoration painted over enamel, XIIIth century. Lustred Islamic ceramic work from Iran

9 MAJOLICA

The word majolica has several meanings. Today it is commonly used to define clay-bodied pottery glazed with high-fired tin-based enamel decoration. In its Italian form—*maiolica*—it used, once, to apply to lustred works imported from Spain by way of Majorca, or manufactured in Italy. For ceramic historians it is the general name for all Italian pottery produced during the Renaissance.

Archaic Italy
The production of lead-glazed pottery had not faltered since the days of the Roman Empire. From the XIIth century up to the XVth century tin glazes were used as well, particularly in central Italy. Works treated

Luca della Robbia, Nativity, *XVth century, enamelled bas-relief (detail)*

in this manner come under the heading *archaic ceramics*. The tin glaze was used parsimoniously on the upper part of the pot, the foot and interior being simply lead-glazed. The most characteristic shapes were the *panata* or *vasella* (vase with a handle and prominent spout), pitchers with tree-lobed spouts and low cups with straight sides. The decoration was drawn with brown, blackish or purplish-blue manganese oxide and coloured with green obtained from copper, with rare touches of blue. The motifs of the design are simple but boldly drawn to very elegant effect. They are taken from vegetables, birds, animals or human figures. Some bunches of grapes, pine-cones and heads are in relief, having first been moulded and then luted on.

The Italian Renaissance
Renaissance potters were inspired by the same ardour to excel as other artists at that time. They were also dependent on the generosity of princely patrons. From household equipment pottery rose in station to become objects of display. Renaissance potters all used the same basic techniques but

each developed his own personal variations which were closely guarded secrets. They had their own chroniclers, who published treatises on the art. Biringuccio (1480 to 1539) was the author of a treatise on pyrotechnics published in 1540. It was during that period that Piccolpasso composed his treatise *Tre Libri del Arte del Vasaio*, which describes the standard majolica techniques and speaks highly of the principal contemporary workshops. In 1758 Passeri published Pesaro's history of majolica.

Potters vied with one another in virtuosity both for forming and decorating: *L'impalliata* was a vase shape composed of five separate pieces stacked on top of each other, which, unstacked, formed a dinner service; it was offered to women in childbed. The *coppa amorata,* complete with a portrait of the beloved, was a pledge of love. *L'alberello* was the traditional container in pharmacies, which in those days were attached to hospitals, convents and princely homes. Large *storied* platters borrowed their subjects from various forms of expression including painting, engraving and even the first published books.

The della Robbia, amongst whom Luca (1400–1482), Andrea (1435–1528) and Giovanni (1469–1529) are the best known, form a class apart. Although they were sculptors they chose ceramic techniques for work in the round on architectural decoration and fixed church furniture (tabernacles and altar-pieces, for example). The latter were treated as bas-reliefs, early examples being enamelled in two colours–white and blue–while later works also display details in yellow and green. Given their dimensions they had to be carved into separate pieces for moulding, in such a way that once reassembled, the joints would show as little as possible. Works by the della Robbia often have secondary decorative motifs–very naturalistic garlands of fruit and leaves modelled in high-relief. The enamel, which is an even milky white, is used in such a novel way that the famous Renaissance art historian, Vasari, attributed the invention of tin-based enamel to Luca della Robbia.

The principal centres of majolica manufacture were in Umbria, Tuscany, the Marches and Romagna; other centres in the rest of Italy were: Orvieto, Deruta, Gubbio,

Florence, Siena, Casteldurante, Urbino, Pesaro, Faenza, Savona, Venice and Caltagirone.

Amongst all these centres of the art we will choose Faenza, Urbino, Gubbio and Deruta, which produced works either remarkable in their own right or exemplary of their kind.

Faenza

Such was the fame of the ceramic ateliers at Faenza, a town in Romagna, that the town's name was given to a type of pottery: faience.

These workshops produced archaic-style tin-glazed pottery similar to that of other Italian centres, and lead-glazed sgraffiato works. At the beginning of the XVth century an Arabian influence can be felt: the design is drawn on tin enamel with manganese oxide, and the accompanying decoration of oak-leaves is thickly coloured with zaffre blue (cobalt oxide) to achieve a relief effect. This style and technique were fairly common in Tuscany at that time.

Gothic foliage motifs appeared around 1470 along with peacock feathers, branches

Faenza Alberello, *circa 1480. 'Gothic foliage' style majolica*

83

and tendrils–and new colours: yellow, orange, red-brown and blue. The first plates bearing allegorical scenes–they were love pledges–date from this period, as do *point engravings* in which colour applied over enamel is scratched lightly to let the ground colour show through. On the *alberelli* profiles of men and women were painted on grounds of blue or of *Gothic foliage*. The main colour-scheme was blue and yellow, the design blue. The dinner service ordered for the marriage of Mathias Corvin, King of Hungary, with Beatrice of Aragon, in 1476, marks the beginning of the storied style which made Urbino's fortune. Like paintings, works in this style show figures against a landscape. At Faenza the storied decoration generally occupied only the centre of the plate, while the rim was decorated with *grotesques*.

Amongst the workshops of which the names have survived are those of Bettini, Dalle Palle, Manara, but the most renowned atelier was the Cà Pirota. It started operating at the end of the XVth century under Paterni Pietro called Pirotto. His sons were named the Pirotti. Their factory-mark was a wheel of fire (rota pyros).

The development, during the XVIth century, of the *beretinno* enamel is attributed to the Cà Pirota: white tin-based enamel was tinted with cobalt before application, which gave it a lavender shade. On this ground a normal colour palette was used, dominated by a harsh blue. By contrast, yellow acquired a special brilliance. The decoration was heightened with *blanc fixe*.

After 1520, *blanc fixe* was also used to draw arabesque motifs on a ground of white enamel. The combination of the two tones of white and different textures gave an effect surprisingly similar to fine embroidery. The taste for such fine work also found expression in the style known as *a la porcellana* which consists of a monochrome blue camaieu decoration of interlaced sprigs and miniature flowers.

Towards the middle of the XVIth century pottery shapes became more complicated displaying embossed convex effects, while the works were divided into sections by gadroons and grooves which were accentuated by the decoration.

Diana and Actaeon, *first half XVIth century. Storied majolica from Deruta*

The religious conflicts of the Reformation and Counter-Reformation, in the second half of the XVIth century were responsible for the appearance of a new style in ceramics: the *compendiaro*–a word which implies a synthesis of, and a harking-back to the art of the past. This style exalts the qualities and subtleties of white tin-based enamel, demonstrating the undesirability of invasive decoration. Common motifs were line-drawings of coats of arms, saints and angels coloured in palest blue or yellow. *Fruttiere* were perforated or formed by a sort of tracery.

Urbino

Urbino, the Marches town of the dukes of Montefeltro and della Rovere, birthplace of Raphael, was in the XVIth century, the uncontested capital of *storied* ceramics. The dukes of Urbino were great patrons of the arts. They attracted many an artist to their courts. Under their patronage ceramics became the province of painters. Each artist explored pictorial possibilities to the utmost of his abilities. The most distinguished ceramic painters were: Francesco Xanto Avelli, de Rovigo, Niccolò Pellipario, his son Guido Fontana, and Alfonso Patanazzi. *Storied* works are all show-pieces. Their subject matter was borrowed from engravings that reproduced works by Raphael, biblical scenes, Aesop's fables and Ovid's Metamorphoses. Engravings by Dürer, Cranach, Mantegna and Giulio Romano also served as models for the painters. On occasion Xanto Avelli even painted political allegories. These ceramic painters, who rivalled each other both in skill and culture, very often signed their works. Storied decoration covered the whole of a work, however complex its form. Some received a final lustre, either in Urbino proper or in Gubbio. Even if one has reservations about the aesthetic quality of such ceramics, one cannot but admire the performance.

Xanto Avelli, The punishment of Rome, *1532. Storied majolica from Urbino*

*Corinthian plate from Etruria, circa 560 B.C.
Painted terracotta*

Gubbio

The Umbrian town of Gubbio, formed, in
the XVIth century, part of the Duchy of
Urbino. It owes its fame to its most celebrated ceramicist: Mastro Giorgio, whose
real name was Giorgio Andreaoli; a native
of Lombardy, he settled in Gubbio in 1498,
having previously worked at Pavia and
Faenza. On his arrival he founded a factory
in collaboration with local potters. He was

made a citizen of Gubbio that same year.
His lustre technique made him famous. Not
only did he lustre his own works, but also
those of potters as celebrated as Niccolò
Pellipario and Xanto Avelli of Urbino. He
obtained the lustre during a third firing.
Certainly this process must already have
been known at Pesaro and Deruta, but the
quality of Mastro Giorgio's lustre is unique,
because of both its transparency and its
inimitable red tone. It was so highly valued
that he added his own signature, in lustre,
with the words *finj de majolica,* to works
already signed by other artists. His first
lustred work is dated 1518; it earned him,
the next year, tax exemption by Pope Leo X,
in recognition of his mastery of majolica.
The difficulties of lustre technique are such,
Piccolpasso assures us, that if one hundred
works are fired no more than six will be un-
packed faultless.

Deruta

Deruta, the small Umbrian town on the
banks of the Tiber, not far from Perugia,
was under the rule of the Pontifical States.
It was unlike other centres of the art in that
its workshops were not supported by

princely patronage–this did not prevent them from producing refined ceramics. In 1475, according to a deed drawn up by a notary, two citizens of Perugia and two potters from Deruta formed a company to carry out experiments in majolica (that is to say, lustre). Deruta must have had an impressive reputation during the XVIth century, because, in 1553, the quality and renown of its production decided the Roman government to grant certain privileges to its inhabitants. Later, widespread marketing and lack of famous patrons, caused the importance of Deruta to be obscured, to such an extent that Passeri attributed most of the works made in Deruta to Pesaro. It is a varied production, but certain shapes and decorations are characteristic.

There are church pavings at the Deruta museum, in St. Peter's church, Perugia, and in a chapel of the Santa-Maria de Spello (which also has wall-frescos by Pinturicchio).

Vases with two handles, a lid and foot, others shaped like pine-cones, *amatorie* cups, salt-cellars, *impalliata* and show-piece plates made at Deruta, differ from works of

Majolica plate from Deruta, late XVth century, early XVIth century

other centres in the style of their decoration, which is sober, serene and extremely graphic with flat areas of colour. The *marli*, or raised rim, was often divided into different compartments. Scales were a favourite theme. Religious subjects were common both for show-pieces and plebeian votive works. Mythological themes were treated with considerable verve. Other

89

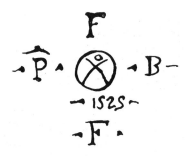

Signature from the 'Cà Pirota' workshop in Faenza

motifs were chosen from a repertoire of fantastic figures including chimera, sphinxes and bird-like serpents. These popular fantasies were often of a satirical nature.

Deruta enamel was a pure white and the colours frank. Designs were often sketched in dark blue. The most exquisite works were painted with blue then given a pearly, pale gold lustre which sometimes inclined towards olive green. *Cantharides* and ruby lustres were rare. The first dated lustred ceramic from Deruta is a moulded relief panel depicting St. Sebastian. It is inscribed 'A.D. 14 de juglio 1501'. So it was in fact made seventeen years earlier than Mastro Giorgio's first lustre. Deruta potters rarely signed their works. However, we know of Francesco d'Urbino (1531–1587) and of a monk who signed his production 'El frate' or 'frate fecit' or again 'el frate pense'; he is thought to have been Giacomo Mancini (1541–1560). In the XVIIth century, Petrus Paulus Mancinus made ceramics from engravings of famous paintings.

As far as popular pottery is concerned, the ex-voto plaques covering the *Madonna dei Bagni* chapel are worth mentioning—they represent Acts of God, the kind of accident which might interrupt a peaceful life, such as lightning, floods, collapsing houses, shying horses, brigands.

Adoration of the Magi, *XVIth century. Storied majolica from central Italy*

10 EUROPE AFTER THE ITALIAN RENAISSANCE

The Renaissance in France

Majolica was taken up all over Europe as an expression of the spirit of the Renaissance. Throughout the XVIth and particularly the XVIIth centuries the style and technique spread; but, at the same time, other types of ceramics appeared.

French potters during the Middle Ages, and up to the XVIth century, continued to use the techniques and processes of their Roman Empire ancestors. They treated imprinted or slip-decorated relief work with lead glaze. Majolica was first produced at Lyon, then taken up at Nîmes, Nevers and

Rustiques figulines, *plate from the school of Bernard Palissy, XVIth century. Glazed terracotta*

Montpelier. The first potters to make high-fired majolica in France were Italian émigrés from Faenza and Urbino. In 1545, Masseot Abaquèsne, one of the earliest known French master-potters, who collaborated with Girolamo della Robbia on the decoration of the Madrid chateau in the Bois de Boulogne, worked in a Rouen atelier staffed by French and Italian workmen. Early examples of French majolica resemble Italian work; however, a new style soon developed which was to make the heyday of factories at Nevers, Rouen and Moustier in the XVIIth and XVIIIth centuries. Grotesqueries made way for *lambrequin, dentelle, broidery* or *rayonnant* decoration, and then for *chinoiserie*. Now the term majolica was replaced by faience. The practice of a third firing became more widespread, particularly in Marseilles, Strasbourg and Sceaux.

Two names must be given places of honour in the history of early French ceramics: those of the potter Bernard Palissy and the Château d'Oiron workshop.

Saint-Porchaire

Madame de Boisy (Hélène d'Hangest), the widow of Arthur Gouffier, François I's late governor, set up and directed a ceramics workshop in her Château d'Oiron. It was active from 1529 in the reign of François I until 1568 in Charles IX's time, when it was destroyed by the wars of religion. She was aided by Jean Bernart and François Charpentier, respectively her secretary/decorator and modeller/potter. They fashioned pottery from a white clay similar to fine faience, which was coated with a slip of even finer white clay. On this they engraved, with a metal tool, an arabesque pattern of interlacing grooves, which were then encrusted with brown, black and red slip. The work was finally glazed with a lead glaze. On the death of Madame de Boisy in 1537, her son Claude Gouffier took over. Works created under Madame de Boisy's direction have a special elegance which is due to the severe soberness of the decoration, while those made under her son's direction, although products of the same technique, are in a different, more exuberant style. Pottery manufactured in this workshop was not intended to be sold but reserved for private use or for offering as gifts. It is known as Henri II faience, Oiron faience or Saint-Porchaire faience.

Bernard Palissy

Bernard Palissy, who was a glass-maker by trade, settled at Saintes in 1539. After a tour of Europe as a journeyman glass-maker he was smitten with such wonder at the sight of a thrown and enamelled clay cup that he determined to discover for himself the secret of enamel. The work in question was probably a white cup from Ferrara. After fifteen years of experimentation, trials and failures, he eventually produced his first works in speckled enamel. But his claim to fame is the *rustic figuline* style. The patronage of the influential Anne de Montmorency, who obtained for him, from Catherine de Medici, the title of *Inventeur du rustique figuline du Roy et de la Royne-Mère,* brought him, a Huguenot, freedom during the religious wars. Once established in Paris, he entered upon a successful career at court. He executed a grotto for Queen Catherine in the Tuileries gardens. His work is noted for the important part played in it by relief in enamelled decoration and for a taste for the naturalistic. The motifs of *rustic figuline* are reptiles, fish and molluscs in conjunction with various sorts of foliage. The clay is hard, compact, pink and heavily fired. The brilliant enamels are thinly coated so as not to soften the relief effect.

Bernard Palissy did not sign his works, but he marked those intended for the Court with *fleurs de lys.* In his memoirs he claims to have destroyed all of his work that he considered imperfect. His is a unique case in the history of ceramics: not only was his style highly original, but his work–always strangely ambiguous, halfway between dream and reality–was inimitable.

Holland–Delft

Ceramics from Delft, the most important centre of Dutch pottery, are the fruits of the love the Dutch artisans bore for art from China and Japan, particularly works in porcelain. Too few of these were available to satisfy the demands of a growing European market, so the Delft workshops united in a corporation to manufacture a tin-based lead-glazed enamel which, decorated with *chinoiserie,* and subjected to a second firing, was sold abusively under the name of porcelain. Delft potters used a fine-grained pale beige-coloured clay which, because of its lightness, formed a fine biscuit. These

Saint-Porchaire cup, first manner, XVIth century. Fine faience with inlaid design

works were either thrown or moulded. They were decorated by brush after pouncing. The design was strengthened with *treck* (a mixture of iron and manganese oxides and blue residue). Some Delft pottery is in monochrome blue, the rest is polychrome, sometimes on a black ground. Colours were first applied to unfired enamel, then, from 1725 onwards, to fired enamel

95

using the triple-firing technique, which makes gilding possible. Delft workshops also decorated porcelain which had been imported from China and Japan. The 'prettiness' of the forms and colours of Delft faience explains its popularity as interior decoration.

It is amusing to note that at the very same period, while the European pottery industry was using Chinese-style decoration, Chinese artisans were decorating their pottery in the European manner.

England

Staffordshire is a naturally privileged region of England as far as ceramics is concerned. It is rich in good clay and wood and coal fuel, and has the advantage of a transport network which encourages commerce. Other parts of England have produced good work, but Staffordshire is the only region to have supported uninterrupted ceramic activity rich in stylistic invention and technical research.

At the end of the XVIth and during the XVIIth century, English potters produced a

'Tulip vase' from Delft, circa 1740. Enamelled faience

good quality tin-glazed faience in the style and using the techniques of Delft-ware majolica. However, the use of tin glaze was only temporary.

During the Middle Ages lead-glazed English pottery was decorated with incised or relief motifs, fillets and pastillage. The use of engobe was common practice. A large part of the ceramic output of this period is said to be in *Cistercian style*.

Slip-ware ceramics

In the XVIIth and XVIIIth centuries potters used slip for decoration in such an original way that works made at this time are called *slip-ware*. The best known slip-ware potters were Thomas Toft and Ralph Simpson; their signatures form part of the decoration. St. George killing the dragon, Adam and Eve, various allegorical themes, heraldry motifs and royal portraits were favourite subjects for decoration. The colours of the clay slips varied from yellow ochre to brown. The design was drawn by pouring liquid slip through a bird's quill onto green-

Archaic English pitcher with lead glaze, XIIIth to XIVth century

hard clay. For plates, the reverse side only was coated with glaze, by sifting on crushed galena (sulphide of lead). Traces of ferruginous matter in the galena resulted in subtle differences in the colouring of the slip. This kind of work was probably completed in a single firing.

The beginning of industrialisation– Wedgwood

Meanwhile, from the end of the XVIIth century in fact, other English potters had been undertaking a number of experiments in forming techniques in an attempt to discover the compositions of the clays used for stoneware and fine faience. These experiments led to the industrialisation of ceramics.

Early research was directed towards the very hard unglazed stoneware, the white and marbled clays first, then red and black stoneware. It was started in 1670 by John Dwight and continued by two brothers, David and Philip Elers, who were born and trained in Germany but emigrated to England at the end of the XVIIth century. These experiments were prompted by the fast spreading fashion for tea-drinking which had recently taken hold in England. The aim was to match the quality of Chinese teapots. The Elers brothers' style of decoration called for the use of metal impression-tools; the design was thus extremely sharp. John and Thomas Astbury, too, used metal seals to apply white clay over coloured grounds. They also made white salt-glazed stoneware. The introduction of slip-casting in plaster moulds, in 1745, was a decisive step in the search for means of reproducing pottery and rationalising its production. The advent of this technique was one of the reasons why, at the end of the XVIIIth century, salt-glazed stoneware was abandoned in favour of fine faience ware.

Thomas Whieldon obtained a successful marbled effect by combining different coloured clays.

Josiah Wedgwood, who worked with Whieldon from 1754 to 1759, improved the composition of the clay used for fine faience cream ware by adding kaolin and feldspar. He was the first potter to use transfers for decorating ceramics. In 1769 he named his factory, which is still active to this day, 'Etruria'. The compositions of his clays are difficult to classify; they are usually referred to by the names he himself chose: porphyry, basalt, Queen's Ware, jasper and biscuit. His love for the then fashionable Neoclassical style can be seen in the many ceramics which display white figures against a blue or tender pink ground.

There was also at that time—the late XVIIIth century—a great vogue for the large series of faience figurines and statuettes modelled by the Wood family.

Stoneware in Germany

German ceramics are particularly interesting because of the predominance of stoneware. Jugs, beer-mugs and bottles were being made from high-fired sandy siliceous clay as far back as the Middle Ages; their frank forms and lack of decoration give them a rough beauty.

Kreussen stoneware was produced in Saxony and Bavaria. The main pottery centres were, however, to be found in the region around the Rhine valley. Stoneware from Flanders and Walloon Belgium bears a distinct likeness to that produced in Germany. It was for a long time known as Flemish stoneware because it appealed to

'Ralph Simpson', slip-ware, plate, late XVIIth century

99

the taste of Flemish collectors. However there are no doubts about its German origins: inscriptions in German dialect and coats of arms of German princes which are part of the ornamentation are proof enough. The First Lady of stoneware history is Jacqueline of Bavaria, the Countess of Hainault, who made stoneware pots in Teylingen Castle in 1424. She threw her production into the moat so as not to be forgotten. The *Jakoba Kannetjes* style is named after her.

Salt glaze was invented in the XVth century. Later, stoneware was also enamelled and gilded, both by and without firing.

The several potter families of Siegburg formed an exclusive trade-guild. They produced unglazed or salt-glazed white stoneware. The subjects they chose for decoration were taken from engravings and were carried out by impression.

Potters at Cologne—whence an important amount of stoneware was exported to Holland, England and France—pooled efforts with their fellow artisans of Frecken to manufacture salt-glazed stoneware in a range of browns, with coarser clay than their Siegburg colleagues. The themes of their decorations were borrowed from prints, or vegetables, masks and coats of arms. Stoneware was manufactured in Cologne up to the XVIIIth century. The most beautiful examples are XVIth century.

The ceramic clay used at Raeren was grey; the glaze—brown in the early days, then later blue—was dabbed on. Cylindrical-bodied pitchers suitable for frieze decoration were the favourite shape. Jan Emens and Balden Mennicks are the best known Raeren potters.

XVIIth century Westerwald stoneware is characterized by an incised decoration of rosettes, palmettes and zigzags on grey clay glazed blue or purplish blue.

Reddish clay was used for Kreussen stoneware, it was given a dark brown glaze, and, as it was decorated with bright enamels and gold, it was fired twice. The exuberant ornamentation was borrowed from popular and religious imagery.

The invention of hard-paste porcelain in Europe
When Marco Polo saw works in porcelain for the first time, during his voyage to China, he was so struck by their pearly

quality that he named them *porcella*, after a highly-valued shell which at that time served as money in the Far East. *Porcella* was mis-rendered *porcelana* and eventually, in English, *porcelain*.

Although it is extremely hard, unscratchable and impermeable, porcelain clay produces forms of amazing finesse, the diaphanous, precious, fragile appearance of which has given rise to passionate admiration and desperate attempts by alchemists to discover its secret.

Strange legends surrounded porcelain crockery from the beginning, among them one attributing to it the power to reveal the presence of poisons—a useful power in those days!

All attempts to imitate this new clay resulted in soft-paste porcelain, which consists of mixtures of vitreous or phosphate frits. The first soft-paste porcelain was manufactured in Florence by Buontalenti in 1574, during the reign of Francesco I de Medici. 38 examples of his work have come down to us. In France at the end

Siegburg beer-mug, middle XVIth century. White stoneware

of the XVIIth century, Chicaneau developed a clay resembling porcelain at St. Cloud. Other similar clays were perfected at Lille, Chantilly, Mennecy-Villeroy and Vincennes, early in the XVIIIth century.

In 1756 the Vincennes works were acquired by Louis XV, at Madame de Pompadour's insistence, and moved to Sèvres, where, in 1760, it became a Royal Factory. Several towns, including Sceaux, Orléans, Arras and Valenciennes were centres of soft-paste porcelain manufacture up to the end of the XVIIIth century.

In England, *Bone China,* containing a phosphate flux, which bears some resemblance to porcelain, was produced at Chelsea (1741), Derby (1751) and Caughley (1756).

The qualities of porcelain are due to the composition of the clay: a mixture of kaolin and petuntse, a feldspathic rock. The first beds were discovered accidentally in Germany—the home of stoneware and, in consequence, of high-temperature firing— in the reign of August the Strong, by an alchemist called Johann Friedrich Böttger. Since he claimed to have manufactured gold, Böttger was ordered to appear before the king at Dresden and placed under the guard of Baron Tschirnhausen. Legend has it that the kaolin beds were discovered when he noticed that his valet had dusted his wig with an unusual mineral powder. He recognised it as being pure kaolin. It had been sold by a man named Schnorr, and came from Aue. In 1709 he was able to announce to the king that he had succeeded in manufacturing a porcelain of such excellent quality that it equalled Far-Eastern ware. The king founded factories, first at Dresden, then at Meissen. It is hard to say whether Böttger and his colleagues were protégés or prisoners. They were obliged on oath to keep all their activities secret. Böttger also invented a red stoneware that was so hard that it could be cut and polished like stone. At the time of his death, in 1719, the Meissen factory had not yet developed a style of its own. It produced copies of Chinese porcelain or silver-ware. Böttger never succeeded in obtaining underglaze blue and only had a limited colour palette. The decoration was sometimes unfired. Early works were in the form of medals, vases, beer-mugs and small statuettes. Underglaze blue was discovered by

Mehlhorn and Köhler in 1720. That year the painter Gregor Höroldt was hired by the factory. It was he who created the style which made Meissen famous. His research into the chemical nature of glazes enabled him to obtain a great variety of colours during a third firing. The painters were forbidden to sign the works that were for sale.

The taste for chinoiserie had completely vanished by 1740. A style peculiar to Meissen had replaced it, which was in some ways influenced by French soft-paste porcelain. The statuette modellers, who helped forge the Meissen style, were Johann Gottlob Kirchner, employed in 1727 and Johann Joachim Kändler, who was employed in 1731.

Of course, the secret could not be kept for long. Deserters from Meissen were responsible for the creation of factories at Vienna in 1717, and Höchst in 1746, then later at Strasbourg and Frankenthal. Other factories started porcelain production in

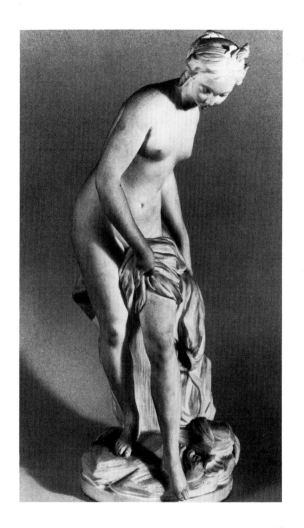

Baigneuse, *after the original by Falconet, 1758.*
Sèvres biscuit-ware

Italy at Venice, Doccia and Naples; in Spain at Buen Retiro, then in Denmark, Holland, Switzerland, Sweden and Russia.

In France, the creation of a factory at Limoges coincided with the discovery of kaolin beds at Saint-Yrieix in 1766. The royal factory at Sèvres which had continued to manufacture soft-paste porcelain, was let into the hard-paste secret just prior to 1770. From then on, until the Revolution, it benefited from privileges by which it was assured exclusive rights on statuette modelling and the use of gold and certain other colours. Paris, Niederwiller, Orléans, Marseilles, Lunéville all created their own factories.

Painted porcelain decoration is usually overglazed, requiring a third firing, but from the end of the XIXth century onwards underglaze was also used. A porcelain surface can be treated in a good many different ways. It has even been made to resemble other materials such as wood, stone and, surprisingly, terracotta.

The industrialisation of porcelain, and an ever increasing division of labour, have caused this form of ceramics to lose favour with art potters.

Cylindrical Maya vase, classical period, IXth–Xth century. Polychrome painted terracotta

11   PRE-COLUMBIAN CERAMICS

The heading pre-Columbian ceramics is intended to cover the entire production of the peoples of the American continent up to the arrival of Europeans. This production was spread out over many thousands of years. The American peoples lived in a variety of climates and had different cultures. We know very little about their history. The European conquest, which destroyed numerous traces of their past, brought an end to the integrity of their cultures. The conquerors were amazed by the strangeness of the works of art of pre-Columbian indians.

In this context Dürer wrote in his *Letters and theoretical Writings:* 'Never, in all my life, have I seen things which thrilled me as much as these objects do. Because I see them as works of a singular art and I was filled with admiration before the subtle ingenuity of men from far-off lands'. Unfortunately Dürer was one of the few Europeans to appreciate the artistic value of these objects. Most only looked at the gold. Genuine interest in pre-Columbian ceramics is recent.

Archaeologists usually accept the following schematized classification (from which North America and Amazonia are absent due to insufficient points of reference):
- Mexico (including Guatemala).
- Central America, which stretches from Honduras to northern Columbia.
- The Andes, subdivided into the northern Andes (Columbia, Ecuador), Central Andes (Peru and Bolivia) and Southern Andes (Argentine and Chile). Peru is itself divided into four regions: north coast, central coast, south coast and Andes.

Pre-Columbian history can be divided into three main periods:
- Pre-classical period, from 1500 B.C. to 200 A.D.
- Classical period, from 200 A.D. to 1000 A.D.
- Post-classical period, from 1000 A.D. to 1521–1532 A.D.

There are two reasons for the typical aspects of pre-Columbian ceramics: the throwing-wheel was not used and pottery surfaces were not glazed. Pottery was modelled by hand or moulded into numerous forms including tripod vases, and anthropomorphic, zoomorphic or cephalomorphic vases. Colours were obtained by engobes or from metal oxides, and sometimes from resins. No kilns have yet been discovered, but this by no means implies that there weren't any. The earliest known terracottas date from the second millennium B.C. They were found at Tlatilco, near Mexico City. The oldest work from the Andes region is thought to be Chavin pottery in Peru, which dates from the first millennium B.C.

Mexico

One can get a good idea of the variety of the ceramic production of the Mexican zone from Aztec art, the *Colima, Jalisco* and *Nayarit* of north-west Mexico and from Mayan works.

A striking characteristic of Aztec pottery is that many works are 'musical'; there are hollow bell-statuettes, instruments like the ocarina, and flutes and whistles decorated with the figures of gods. Long-handled censer-like objects, pipes and *pintaderas* were also made in ceramics, the latter serving to apply body-paint. Most of these works were modelled by hand, but the statuettes were moulded. Aztec ceramics only just antedated the conquest and vanished at the shock of the confrontation.

Colima, Nayarit and *Jalisco* ceramics from north-west Mexico, had, during the classical and post-classical periods all the expressive and narrative qualities of sculpture. Works from these three cultures differ in details of clothing and colour-schemes. The dimensions of the figures vary between four and a score inches high; they were modelled—the clay-body was fairly heavy. They represent members of their society and illustrate scenes from everyday life, showing musicians, dancers, warriors, prisoners, the sick and crippled, women in childbirth, people playing games and working, animals; but gods are excluded.

The style of the cylindrical vases decorated with painted figures which were found in Mayan regions is unique. The decoration consists of groups of figures forming a frieze or separated from each other by vertical strips of hieroglyphics. The red, yellow ochre, white and black figures are painted on an orange ground. Other Mayan vases have a sgraffiato decoration. When the clay had been encrusted with coloured engobe (usually orange) it was burnished.

Central America
Ceramics from central America in general and particularly *Nicoya* pottery, are distinguished by their vivid polychrome decoration. These stylized ornamentations, often in relief, obtained by pouncing or even embossing, are most often red or black against a creamy white ground. The feet of tripods are, save rare exceptions, hollow and designed as bells.

Peru
Peruvian pottery is without doubt the most exquisite of all work from pre-Columbian America. Style and technique are inseparable. The earliest works were found in the region of the north coast. They are products of the *Chavin* culture. The *stirrup* vase shape, which was a favourite with Peruvian potters, had already been developed.

'Jalisco' figurine, modelled terracotta

The clay—usually black, but sometimes brown or red—was fired in a reducing atmosphere. Its partially burnished surface is decorated with stylized motifs which have been incised, obtained by reworking pastillage or modelled.

Mochica ceramics are from the same region. They are thought to have been made at the beginning of our Christian era. They were fired in an oxidising atmosphere. These pots, made from fairly pure clay, are thin-sided and burnished. Engobes provide the colour-scheme which is restrained to two tones: white and terracotta-red or white and purple-brown. The forms were moulded in several pieces and finished by hand. The handle is nearly always in *stirrup* style. The decoration is painted and stylized, the drawing flat, or else in relief heightened by colour. The motifs borrowed from everyday life include hunting and fishing scenes, figures, realistic portraits, and animals. These works, which were recovered from burial places, are an important source of information on the lives and habits of American Indians.

Also from the same region, but dating from the later town-building period (between 1200 and 1450) are the Chimu ceramics. They are made from compact well-fired clay, coloured red or white by firing in a reducing atmosphere. The satin-like appearance of the surface is due to burnishing before firing. Painted ornamentation is rare. The object and its decoration are one and the same thing; they are either obtained by moulding or by imprinting and incision. Stirrup vases are still common, but the portraiture is less realistic than in Mochica pottery.

The most unexpected form is the double-bellied whistling-vase which consists of two communicating bellies, one of which is round and topped by an elongated spout while the other is square and acts as a support for various figures. The whistle is situated in a handle which joins the spout to one of the figure's backs. It is supposed that these vases were reserved for use during funerals as when filled and shaken they emit a piercing whistle accompanied by a melancholy rattle.

The *Caves of Paraca* pottery, which dates from before our era, deserves special

Globular double-spouted 'Nazca' vase, classical period, first millennium A.D. Polychrome terracotta

'Nicoya' tripod cup with bells. Polychrome terra-cotta

mention. The red, brown or blackish pot-body is well fired, although the clay has in some cases been poorly prepared. The point-engraved decoration was filled with a whitish clay, then coloured with lively brilliant pigments obtained from resins, which are easily mistaken for enamel. This pottery is amongst the earliest from the south coast of Peru; it comes from the same region as the *Nazca* ceramics.

Nazca ceramics were either moulded or modelled satiny-surfaced flat bowls, goblets and globular-bellied double-spouted vases with flat handles. Vase-bases are usually convex. The very fine pot-body is rosy-ochre in colour. The seven or eight tone polychrome ornamentation, which can be found nowhere else in pre-Columbian ceramics, was obtained by the application of engobes over previously burnished clay. The forms it decorates are simple and practically without any relief. Favourite themes for decoration are stylized animals and gods. The drawings are outlined in umber. The highly contrasted design and polychromy, far from detracting from the form, make it come alive. These painted images are suggestive of some sort of poetical trance. They bring to mind one of the myths collected by Levi-Strauss: 'There was once a young woman who was clumsy with her hands. She made formless pottery. Her sisters-in-law scornfully coated her head with clay, instructing her to fire it in place of a pot.

'One day an old woman appeared before her and listened to the tale of her misfortunes. She was a good fairy, who taught her to fashion magnificent pots. On leaving she informed the young woman that henceforth she would appear to her in the form of a serpent which the young woman must

'Chimu' double-bellied whistling vase, post-classical period, XIIth–XIIIth century. Burnished black clay

A view of the same vase broken open, showing the workings of the whistle

embrace without repugnance. The young woman obeyed her instructions, and the serpent changed immediately into a fairy who showed her ward how to paint pottery: She took some white clay and covered the pots with an even coating. Then she traced beautiful designs of all kinds with yellow, brown and roucou (urucu: bixa orellana) clay and said to the young woman: 'There are two ways of painting—Indian painting and flower-painting. We call Indian painting that which traces the head of the lizard, the Way of the Great Serpent, a pimento branch, the breast of Boyusu, the rainbow serpent; the latter consists in painting flowers.'

This myth from the Amazonian tribes, which could so easily apply to Nazca pottery, is illustrative of the great Oneness of the Indian soul.

Sung cup and stand, XIth–XIIth century. 'Ts'ing-pai' glazed porcelain

12 THE FAR EAST

Porcelain, which was imported into Europe after the Renaissance and stimulated so much stylistic and technical research, only represents one aspect of Far Eastern ceramics. High-temperature firing and glazing are very old-established techniques in the Far East. Pots were vitrified with lead glaze and with alcaline or feldspathic couvertes even before our era. The quality of the clays and the way they were combined with couverte or glaze makes it difficult to differentiate between stoneware, Oriental stoneware and porcelain. Whiteness and transparency are not the only qualities of porcelain. Asiatics consider its feel, texture and sonority to be equally important. Most clays and couvertes were fired at high temperatures (1300° to 1400°C); they are called *high-fired glaces*. The firing of glaze over couverte, which is carried out at a lower temperature is a *semi-high-firing*. The *low-firing*, or *muffle-firing* used for enamels is performed at about 800°C. Thus *high-firing* and *low-firing* temperatures do not correspond to those reached for European ceramics. Finally we should remember that throughout the Far East, across the vast territory that comprises China, Korea, Indochina and Japan, no distinction is drawn between the major and minor arts and ceramics have always been held in high esteem.

China
Neolithic pottery first made its appearance in the Yellow River basin during the third millennium B.C. It was either formed entirely by hand, by coiling, and cord decorated; or formed by hand and finished on a wheel. It was painted with a polychrome decoration. Examples of the first method are made from grey clay, the others from red clay. Much more rarely finebodied, black, burnished pots have been found which were fully fashioned on a throwing-wheel.

The first glazed surfaces probably date from the Han Dynasty (206 B.C.–220 A.D.), or perhaps from the Warring States

Sung bowl, XIth–XIIth century. Stoneware coated with brown glaze, decoration of leaves

period (403–221 B.C.). They owe their elegance to their restrained simplicity. The clays, which are red or blue-grey, have the characteristics of stoneware and proto-porcelain. The most widely-known works are the *Yueh celadons* with their feldspathic couvertes.

Ceramics were mainly intended for funerary use: urns with covers, large jars, *Hu* vases, boxes with motifs in moulded relief, tripods and *Ming-ch'i* figurines all accompanied the departed to remind him of various aspects of life.

The T'ang Dynasty (618–907) and the Five Dynasties (907–960) were a great period of Chinese ceramics as well as a time of political expansion, prosperity and active trade with Persia and the Middle East. Fragments of T'ang pottery have been found at Samarra and at Fostat in Egypt. Significantly, certain T'ang statuettes represent travelling merchants.

During this period lead-glazed ceramics were formed in clay, stoneware or porcelain and decorated with a polychrome colour-scheme comprising a white, a green, a reddish-brown ochre and, more rarely, a blue. Potters exploited the fluid quality of glaze to create effects of texture. Blobs of colour became decorative motifs. The bases of these works were usually left unglazed. Pottery experts have been unable to discover whether the glaze was amalgamated with the colour or applied after it. On certain plates pigments have been used to colour floral motifs drawn in sgraffiato. Glaze–unlike the feldspathic couverte used for white pottery and celadon–does not fuse into the clay and is liable to flake off.

A fondness for polychrome decoration led some T'ang potters to create works in marbled clay. Ceramics were also a form of sculpture. The Ming-ch'i figurines discovered in tombs were, during successive periods of time, first painted with unfired colours, then glazed and finally coated with feldspathic couverte. They represent a variety of subjects including demoniacal figures, legendary guardians, warriors, cleverly caricatured Armenian, Jewish or Persian merchants, musicians, dancing girls and jugglers, camels and horses, all forming lively tableaux.

China entered into a period of isolationism with the Sung Dynasty (960–1276). Although the nomadic invasions forced the Chinese to move their capital south, they reaped the benefit of a long period of prosperity, and developed the sort of philosophy of life that is beneficial to a great increase in artistic activity. Marco Polo's voyage took place during the Southern Sung period.

Ming five-colour bottle-vase, reign of Wan-Li, 1573–1619. Porcelain with enamel decoration (detail)

In the north, where the influence of Confucianism was felt strongly, we find certain details of technique which are peculiar to that region: there was a predilection for stoneware; works were given a light film of white engobe before being completely glazed; kilns were constructed with large rounded-roofed chambers fitted with a rear chimney and were fired with coal.

In the south where Zen Buddhism was predominant, potters were drawn to porcelain; couverte was applied without engobe; large-sized kilns were constructed on the slope of a hillside–they consisted of a series of chambers and were fired with wood.

Works from the north and south vary in style. We now group them according to their origin. They were packed in *saggars* on *spurs* or placed upside down on a kaolin support. In the latter case the lip of the pot loses its glaze.

The typical shapes of Sung period pottery are: ewers, bowls, bowls with lobed rims, vases with large flared necks, small-necked *Mei-p'ing* vases and head-rests.

The famous celadon ware thus named after its pale blue-green jade colour, was fired in a reducing atmosphere with a feldspathic couverte containing traces of ferruginous matter. When applied to pots decorated by incision, combing or impression, this coating gives a variety of nuances depending on its thickness. The ivory-coloured white Sung ware is also famous for its delicate glazes. Works in the *clair de lune* or *flambé* styles are usually stoneware glazed with contrasting colours (blue, grey, purple and purple-blue).

The *temmoku,* which are known by their Japanese name because of the admiration in which they were held by lovers of the tea-ceremony, have a remarkable dark, almost black glaze, which was applied to extremely coarse-textured stoneware. The glazes are of many types: iris, streaked, *hare fur, partridge feather, oil-spot* or *tortoise-shell.* In some cases decoration was obtained by sticking the leaves of trees to the glaze where their ashes left a coloured imprint.

Other Sung works have a design drawn in sgraffiato through a black engobe covering a ground of white engobe; all coated with a transparent glaze. Crackle is another decorative effect which can be obtained deliberately, and it is made more apparent by rubbing in colour after firing.

Sung potters were exceptionally skilled. They mastered all the ceramic techniques and combined them to brilliant effect and

Globular T'ang jar with moulded feet, VIIth–VIIIth century. 'Three-colour' pottery with lead glaze

117

Korean 'mei-p'ing' vase, Koryŏ period (918–1392). Porcelain stoneware with celadon glaze over inlaid white design

with great art. Striking examples of this mastery are those rare works which we find superimposed on reddish stoneware: a white engobe, painted decoration (peony leaves), a transparent glaze and a tinted glaze. The subtleties of texture and colour thus obtained are truly extraordinary.

After the Mongol Yuan Dynasty, the country returned to Chinese rule under the Ming Dynasty (1368–1664). The imperial factory at King-Tö-Tchen was founded in 1369. It rapidly became the leading manufacturer of porcelain. Its wares were exported throughout the world. The best-known Ming porcelain is the blue and white ware, with blue animals and plants painted on a white ground. It was the main inspiration for European Delft ware. The blue varies with the source of its cobalt oxide. Another equally popular style consisted of a red underglaze decoration on a white ground. The red was obtained from copper by firing in a reducing atmosphere. In the middle of the XVIth century a new *five-colour* porcelain appeared. The colours are obtained from enamel overglaze, only blue remained underglaze.

The use of *semi-high-fired* enamels makes it possible to obtain a good number of colour combinations. It was pottery produced during the Ming period that gave Europeans the taste for *chinoiserie*. From the XVIth century onwards potters in the Kiang Sou region, on the Yellow Sea, produced burnished stoneware teapots in a variety of browns, which later inspired English potters. During the Ming Dynasty potters started the practice of dating works by marking them with the reign of the emperor.

Around the year 1700 during the Manchurian Ts'ing Dynasty (1644–1912), the Emperor K'ang-hi re-opened the imperial factory. Technically its production is perfect, but aesthetically there is a decline in expressive force. Nevertheless certain effects like *sang de bœuf*, flammé, coloured enamels on black ground or powdered colours have given rise to works of great quality.

Korea

Ceramics is an ancient art in Korea. Technically it resembles that of China, but it differs both in spirit and in some of the processes used.

The three kingdoms of Kokuryŏ, Paekche and Silla were unified in 668 A.D. and formed what was once called Great Silla. At that period Buddhism had a strong influence on the flowering of the arts. But it was not until the Koryŏ period (918–1392) that Korean potters, who were particularly interested in celadons, produced their most beautiful work, which was admired even by Chinese connoisseurs of the Sung period. During the Yi Dynasty (1392–1910) the reputation of Korean potters remained strong; they played an important role in the history of Japanese ceramics at the end of the XVIth century; they were in fact moved forcibly to Japan and once there obliged to practise their art and hand on their techniques to their conquerors.

With their muted colours and delicate variations of tone, Korean celadons are imbued with an attractive melancholy stillness. 'Whenever I behold an example of Korean pottery, I am confronted with everlasting nothingness, the source of all beauty, purity and depth', said the Japanese connoisseur Uchiyama.

Celadon glazes, fired at high temperatures, were used for a variety of shapes and styles of decoration, by which Korean work is now classified: undecorated celadon with plain glaze, incised celadons, celadons with bas-relief decoration, with modelled and fretted decoration, with modelled figures, incrustation, gilding, red decoration obtained from copper, or painted ornamentation. Celadon glaze was also used to coat works in red and white marbled clay, and

Detail of inlay (see p. 118)

pots treated with black engobe rich in iron which are known as *Koryŏ black* or *Koryŏ temmoku.*

The technique for incrustation is as follows: a design is incised quite deeply in green-hard clay; the grooves thus obtained are filled with white or reddish-brown slip. The surface is smoothed down thoroughly. Finally the glaze is applied. Some experts claim that these works were completed in a single firing, others insist that two firings were necessary. It has been observed that the shrinkages of the various types of clay vary in proportion to the importance of the incrustation, and can on occasion cause it to crack.

Japan

Japanese ceramics have been so closely linked to the tea-ceremony, which has been performed since the XIIIth century, and to the techniques imported by Korean potters, that the originality of earlier pottery tends to be forgotten. Cord-decorated Jōmōn pottery (third millennium to IInd century B.C.) and the finer-bodied Vayoi ceramics (IIIrd century B.C. to Vth century A.D.) are extraordinarily lively. They were both formed by hand and fired in the open. Cultural exchanges with the Chinese mainland brought technical improvements including the throwing-wheel and the bank-kiln which was in use during the Sueki period (Vth century–middle IXth century A.D.), and the first couvertes and glazes (many of them initially obtained by accident).

There is a legend that during the Kamakura period (1180–1330), a Buddhist monk Tōshirō, who was a potter from Seto, stayed in China and learned the techniques of that country's potters. The story goes that he took large quantities of raw material home with him, before searching for them on Japanese soil. Black glazed *temmoku*, *autumn leaf* glazes and the almost exclusive use of stoneware are typical of this period. Six centres were known for their ceramics: Tokanabe, Shigaraki, Tamba, Bizen, Echizen and Seto; they were called the 'six ancient kilns of Japan'. The name of Seto, where pottery was both glazed (intentionally) and decorated, eventually became the generic term for pottery, stoneware and porcelain–*seto-mono*.

The repercussions of various events which occured during the XVth and XVIth centuries left their mark on the history of ceramics. Endless civil wars forced craftsmen to flee, abandoning their kilns only to rebuild others elsewhere. The Seto kiln was reconstructed at Mono. The tea-ceremony, which was in nature both social and ritual was systematized. It inspired the creation of a new style of pottery which broke with tradition. The masters of tea *(Tchaiins)* sought out the most talented potters, and sometimes gave their names to the potter's production. *Oribe* pottery, for instance, is called after the master Furuta Oribe. The history of *Raku* ware from the second half of the XVIth century, illustrates the importance of both tea and ceramics: Rikyu, the tea master, introduced Chōjirō, a potter who had been born in Korea, to the military leader Hideyoshi. Hideyoshi, in recognition of the beauty of Chōjirō's pottery, presented him with a seal bearing the word *Raku,* which signifies pleasure and sensual enjoyment. This mark was later used by Chōjirō's descendants, who, true to the Japanese tradition, were also potters.

The relationship which grew up between

Japanese tea-ceremony boxes (cha-ire), XIXth century. Stoneware with a play of glazes

the masters of tea and potters favoured an individualistic approach to ceramics which permitted works of great originality. These, notwithstanding, have many points in common; stoneware was the most popular style; potters strove for asymmetry; surface treatments tended to enhance the natural appearance of the clay. Crackled effects, cracks, holes, grain and rough patches were not the result of poor craftsmanship, they were, rather, so many means for the potter to give way, through a perfectly finished object, to the primitive instinct for violence and to rape the clay.

13 CONTEMPORARY CERAMICS

The spectacular blossoming of contemporary ceramics has many different roots which are difficult to analyse because of the social upheavals of the last fifty years and the changeable currents of aesthetic criticism. It is probably not inaccurate to suggest that this renewed interest in pottery springs to a large extent from a reaction against industrialization and is part of the common reflex in developed countries towards individualism and Nature. Artists everywhere are trying to re-establish a direct contact with elementary matter.

Elisabeth Langsch, enamelled ceramic wall for a private swimming-pool at Kilchberg (p. 128)

The fashion for stoneware and the fascination it holds for potters in parts of the world where, until now, it had scarcely been known, can be explained, we suggest, precisely by its rough and unfinished appearance which dispenses with superfluous decoration, and exalts the qualities of clay, of glaze or of slip.

Industry provides potters today with kilns that produce predictable results and with basic materials unlikely to cause unpleasant surprises. Techniques are no longer tied to the raw materials and traditions of a given region. They have become universal. They can be found everywhere.

Freed, now, from many technical limitations, art potters work in conditions of great artistic freedom. Today, ceramics are definitively considered as unique works, vehicles for personal self-expression, whereas in the past, with the exception of

◁ *Ursula Scheid, Vase 1969. Porcelain with orange-brown glaze*

Dome of the Shah's mosque at Ispahan. Polychrome enamelled facing-plaques

126

works by a few great masters, pottery was closely tied to one people, one religion, one civilisation or dynasty.

Today's individualistic approach to ceramics has lured many a distinguished painter, like Gauguin, Braque, Chagall, Léger, Derain, Matisse, Miró and Picasso into trying their hand at the art (thus giving short shrift to the ridiculous distinction between 'major' and 'minor' art forms). A place of honour must be reserved for Picasso, for he truly adopted ceramics as his main means of expression during a whole period of his creative life–and not content with limiting himself to carrying out a painter's work on ceramic ground he succeeded in creating works in which form and decoration are perfectly integrated.

The main interest of these painters' experiments in pottery lies in the fact that it is essentially thanks to them that ceramics, then dying of industrialization, was reanimated and given fresh significance.

But since today all everyday objects have become industrialized, art potters have had to find new outlets for their creativity. A possible answer lies in the integration of ceramics with architecture, harking back to a very ancient practice. It certainly cannot be denied that the permanent quality of ceramics and the possibilities they offer for relief work and colour make them ideal decoration for towns.

We are too close to contemporary experiments in pottery to see them in proper perspective, and that, anyway, is an art critic's job. But we rejoice in the thought that they present today's potters with almost unlimited scope for artistic expression.

Pablo Picasso, The Owl, *1952. Modelled terracotta with painted decoration*

Elisabeth Langsch, enamelled ceramic wall for a private swimming-pool at Kilchberg (p. 128)

SYNOPSIS

Ceramics	The Arts	General
Circa 6000 B.C.		
Elam: first pottery, sometimes painted		Elam: cereals, stockbreeding
6000 to 5000 B.C.		
Iran, Hajji Firuz: pottery with geometric painted decoration	Anatolia: steatopygous statuettes of unfired clay	
Iran, Islamailabad: red pottery with black painted decoration	Islamailabad: glass-paste necklaces	
5000 to 4000 B.C.		
Iran, Kara Tepe: kiln formed of clay		Probable beginnings of writing in Egypt
4000 to 3000 B.C.		
Iran, Baku: kiln with separate chambers		
Sumer, Erech: light-coloured thrown and burnished pottery; tack mosaic of painted terracotta	Sumer, Erech: white temple and ziggurat	Gilgamesh, hero-king of Sumer (Mesopotamia). Tablets with picturewriting
Japan: Jōmōn pottery		Egypt: first dynasties
Susa: goblets with stylized painted decoration		Mexico: maize cultivation
		Europe: first use of copper
3000 to 2000 B.C.		
Iran, Beluchistan: thrown pottery	Sumer, sculpture: *gudea worshipping;* Gold-work, Standard of Ur	Elam: proto-Elamite writing
Egypt, Sakkara: ceramic wall-facing in the tomb of the pharaoh Zoser	Egypt: great pyramids of Cheops, Chephren and Mycerinus; Gizeh sphinx; sculpture: crouched scribe	Egypt: Thinite period; Memphite age or Old Kingdom
China: Yang-chao, Longchan, Hiang-T'un pottery		America: cotton textiles
		Peru: first agriculture

Ceramics	The Arts	General

2000 to 1000 B.C.

Mesopotamia and Egypt: first vitrified glazes
Susa: enamelled wall-panels
Crete: Kamares pottery, snake-goddess figurines; 'naturalist' pottery
Greece: proto-geometric pottery
Korea: comb-decorated pottery
Mexico: Tlatilco pottery
Peru: 'Chavin' pottery

Mesopotamia, Mari: *Goddess with spouting vase*
Egypt: obelisks at Luxor Karnak temples
Crete: Cnossos palace
Mycenae: Lions gate
Israel: Jerusalem temple
China: Chang bronzes

Erech becomes Babylon
Egypt: Middle Kingdom, New Kingdom; Rameses II, Akhenaten, Tutankhamen
Asia Minor: Hittite empire
Trojan war
Israel: Saul, David, Solomon

Europe: Iron Age

1000 to 600 B.C.

Assyria, Khorsabad: enamelled panels in palace of Sargon II
Greece: geometric, corinthian and proto-Corinthian pottery
Italy: Villanovan urns
Etruria: 'bucchero sottile'

Assyria: Khorsabad palace

Greece: Doric temple at Delphi sculpture: Delos lions
Homeric poems

Carthage founded
Rome founded
Solon Athenian legislator

Early Etruscan civilization

600 to 500 B.C.

Babylon: enamelled brick walls in Nebuchadnezzar's palace
Susa: enamelled panels in the palaces of Darius and Artaxerxes
Greece: black and red figure painted pottery. Exekias, Sophilos, Klitias, Ergotimos, Euphronius
Etruria: Apollo of Veii

Greece: Paestum temple, Ionic Artemisium temple at Ephesus; sculpture: Selinus metopes, archaic korai
Italy: Capestrano warrior
Etruria: Lionesses tomb Tarquinian bulls. *Capitoline She-wolf,* Etrusco-Roman bronze

Jews deported to Babylon

Egypt conquered by Cambyses
Greece: first panathenaea

Foundation of the Roman Republic and expulsion of Etruscan Tarquins

500 to 400 B.C.

Panaitios, Douris, Hermonax, Meidias

Construction of Parthenon and doric temples at Paestum and

Pericles
Socrates

Ceramics	The Arts	General
White-ground lekythos vases	Agrigentom. Delphic Oracle.	Xerxes defeated at Salamis
China: first glazes	Phidias. Aeschylus' tragedies.	China: Warring States
Etruria: 'bucchero pesante'	Etruria: Tarquinian tomb paintings	Dynasty (481–221)
400 to 300 B.C.		
Magna Graecia: pottery in Apulia	Greece: Scopas sculpts. Plato	Alexander conquers Egypt
Greece: Tanagra terracottas	Etruria: *Portrait of young Velia*	The Gauls take Rome
Peru: 'paracas cavernas' pottery	at Tarquinia	
300 to our era		
Megara cups with relief		End of Etruscan independence
decoration		China: construction of the
Japan: Yayoi pottery	*Victory of Samothrace*	Great Wall
Rome: 'aretina' and lead-glazed	*Lacoon sculpture*	Victory of Rome over Carthage
pottery		Death of Caesar
1st century A.D.		
Early sigillated pottery in Gaul	Rome: construction of coliseum	Rome burns (64 A.D.)
Peru: first 'Mochica' and	Peru: Pucara temple,	Temple destroyed at Jerusalem
'Nazca' pottery	pyramids constructed	
Circa 100 A.D.		
Korea: Silla pottery		
Circa 200 A.D.		
China: first Yueh celadons	Classical period in America	China: the Six Dynasties
		(221–581)
Vth century		
Japan: early Sueki pottery,	China: Yun Kang grottos	Sack of Rome by Alaric
underground kiln, accidental	Byzantine art: Galla Placidia	End of the Roman Empire
glazing, wheel	mausoleum, Ravenna	
VIIth century		
China: early glazed T'ang pottery	China: Long Men sculptured	China: T'ang Dynasty (618–906)
Japan: glazed Nara pottery	grottos	The Hejira
	Japan: gilt bronze sculpture	
	at Nara	

Ceramics	The Arts	General
VIIIth century		
Early archaic Islamic sculpture	Kairouan: mosque	
Japan: Nara pottery still going strong	Cordova: Great Mosque	
	Japan: the Emperor Shomu bequeaths collection to the Todaiji temple at Nara	Council of Nicaea
Mexico: Tepeu Mayan pottery		
IX to XIIth centuries		
Korea: celadons	China: painted landscapes	Coronation of Charlemagne
China: Northern Sung pottery	Europe: Cluny Abbey; Vezelay, Pisa, S. Ambrogio, Milan cathedrals	Sung Dynasty (960–1276)
	America: early postclassical period	
1000		
Persia: Minai ceramics	Bayeux tapestry	Japan: beginning of Kamakura period
Italy: early 'archaic' pottery		
XIIIth century		
Persia: perforated pottery	Spain: work starts on Granada Alhambra	Inquisition instituted
Spain: Malaga pottery		Fall of Acre
Mexico: Toltec pottery	Italy: Cavallini, Cimabue, Giotto, Dante	Marco Polo's voyage
Peru: early 'Chimu' pottery		
China: Sung porcelain, bank-kilns	Peru: 'Chimu' town: Chanchan	Peru: early town-building period
Japan: six ancient kilns	France: Chartres stained-glass	Japan: introduction of the tea-ceremony
XIVth century		
Spain: lustred ceramics from Valencia and Manises	Italy: P. and A. Lorenzetti	The Popes in Avignon
Japan: glazed undecorated stoneware	China: K'ai-fon-fou iron pagoda	China: Ming Dynasty
Korea: white porcelain		
Mexico: Aztec ceramics	Mexico: statue of the goddess *Coatlicue*	Foundation of Tenochtitlan

Ceramics	The Arts	General
XVth century		
Spain: Alhambra vase made in Malaga	Italy: Paolo Uccello, Piero della Francesca, Botticelli, Pinturicchio, Mantegna, Leonardo da Vinci, Michelangelo, Raphael. Brunelleschi builds the dome of Santa Maria del Fiore, Florence	
1431– 1437 Italy: Luca della Robbia models the 'cantoria' for the Florence cathedral		Death of Joan of Arc
Majolica manufactured throughout Italy		
Faenza: 'Gothic foliage' style, early storied pottery		Duke Frederick of Monfeltro builds his Urbino palace
Germany: salt-glazed stoneware Jacqueline of Bavaria		
Asia Minor: Isnik ceramics	Asia Minor: Bayezid mosque at Istanbul	Constantinople taken by Mahomet II (1453)
China: blue and white Ming porcelain	China: Ming tombs	Christopher Columbus discovers the West Indies
Korea: blue and white Yi porcelain		
1501 Faenza: 'Berettino' enamel at Cà Pirota workshop; quarter decoration; 'compendiario' style; Urbino potters: Xanto Avelli, G. Fontana: storied style	St. Peter's of Rome reconstructed by Bramante Michelangelo: *David* (1502) Leonardo da Vinci: *Mona Lisa*	
First dated lustred work from Deruta	Dürer: *Melancholy*	Death of Pope Alexander VI Borgia Francois Ier, king of France
1518 Gubbio: Mastro Giorgio's first lustred work	Raphael decorates the Vatican Château de Chambord	Luther excommunicated
1529 Mme de Boisy founds the Château d'Oiron workshop (St-Porchaire pottery)		

Ceramics	The Arts	General
1539 B. Palissy starts work at Saintes		Calvin leaves France
1540 Piccolpasso's *Treatise*		Pizaro undertakes the conquest
Biringuccio's *Treatise* published	Michelangelo: *The Last Judgement*	of Peru
		Atahualpa, last Inca, assassinated
1545 Masseot Abaquènes working at	Château de Madrid in Bois de	Cortez conquers Mexico
Rouen	Boulogne, Paris	St. Bartholomew Massacre
1574 Medici soft-paste porcelain		
Germany: Cologne stoneware	El Greco: *Dream of Philip II*	
China: five-colour porcelain,		Japan: Tea-ceremony
Kiang Sou burnished stoneware	Shakespeare	systematized
Japan: Mino ceramics, Oribe,	Japan: Kano painting school	Hideyoshi starts leading his
Raku		warriors on expeditions into Korea
Peru: Inca ceramics	America: colonial period	
XVIIth century	Caravaggio	
France: Nevers, Rouen,		Dutch East India Company
Moustiers pottery	Rubens	created
Holland: Delft faience	van Dyck	Louis XIV, king of France
England: Slip-ware pottery,	Hals	China: Ts'ing Dynasty
Thomas Toft, Ralph Simpson	Rembrandt	(1644–1912)
Germany: Westerwald stoneware	Château de Versailles	Edict of Nantes revoked
Japan: Himari porcelain	Monteverdi	
China: '*Mille Fleurs*' porcelain	Molière	
1709 Germany: hard-paste porcelain	Watteau	Louis XIV dies
invented by Böttger	Bach	Louis XV, king of France
1720 G. Höroldt creates the Meissen	Rousseau	
style	Fragonard	
	Couperin	
1725 Delft: third-firing decoration	Voltaire	
1745 Slip-casting introduced in England		
1750 'in the biscuit' Sèvres ceramics		
invented by Bachelier		

Ceramics	The Arts	General
1758 Passeri publishes his Treatise on Pesaro ceramics		
1760 La Manufacture de Sèvres becomes royal	Rousseau's *L'Emile*	Louis XVI, king of France United States become independent Bastille destroyed
1768 Kaolin discovered in France		
1769 Wedgwood founds 'Etruria' factory China: pottery exported to Europe 'Flamme' and powdered-colour ceramics	Goya: *Maya desnuda*	Rosetta stone discovered during the Egyptian Campaign
XIXth century Industrial ceramics, eclectic styles, popular and patriotic pottery	Ingres, Delacroix, Corot, Courbet Napoleon III buys the Campana collection. The Impressionists	Napoleon crowned (1804) End of feudality in Japan
Circa 1900 *Belle Epoque* pottery: E. Gallé, H. S. Lerche, Rosenburg	'Fauves' at the Salon d'automne, Paris	
1908 International Ceramics Museum founded at Faenza by G. Ballardini	Cubism: Braque, Picasso International Exhibition of Decorative Arts, Paris 1925, marks end of 1900 style	Russian Revolution Second World War Declaration of the Rights of Man
1949– Picasso creates pottery at 1971 Vallauris Miró works with Artigas Matisse decorates the Chapelle de Vence Contemporary trends in ceramics become known through a series of international exhibitions	Corbusier: *La chapelle de Ronchamp*	

GLOSSARY OF TECHNICAL TERMS

Acroter. Corner-decoration of Etruscan temples.

Alberello. Tall chemist's vase with a thin waist.

Antefix. Ornament covering the ends of roof-tiles on Etruscan buildings.

Azulejos. Wall-base tiles of Hispano-Mauresque and Islamic buildings.

Beating. A forming technique consisting of raising potwalls by beating on the outside against an object held inside the pot wall. Alternatively preparing clay by beating out air-bubbles.

Biscuit. Formed clay which has undergone a first firing.

Bucchero. Black, burnished Etruscan pot.

Canopic vases. Egyptian vases containing the remains of the dead. Etruscan vases containing the ashes of the dead, oval in form with a modelled lid portraying the features of the deceased and his arms.

Celadon. Glaze of certain Far-Eastern ceramics with subtle variations in colour between green, olive, blue and jade. The name was coined by the French, as the colours reminded them of the shepherd Celadon's ribbons in the painting *L'Astrée*.

Cha-ire. Small scale pot for powdered tea-leaves, usually stoneware lined with precious cloth.

Chamotte. Crushed terracotta mixed with unfired clay.

Champleve. Technique consisting of hollowing out the areas between the lines of a design and inlaying them with vitrifiable material. A technique borrowed from metal enamel work.

Cha-wan. Bowl for infusing tea.

Coiling. Hand forming technique: a sausage of clay is coiled round and up to form a pot.

Colima, Jalisco, Nayarit. Three regions of Mexico which have given their names to three types of pre-Columbian ceramics.

Combing. Decorating ceramics by incising parallel lines in the unfired clay.

Cord decoration. Decoration obtained by pressing cords into wet clay.

Couverte. French term for glaze of high-fired stoneware and porcelain, of composition similar to and compatible with the pot-body.

Crackle. An accidental or intentional effect of minute cracks in a glaze.

Cuerda Seca. Method of preventing colours from running into each other.

De-flocculent. Agent added to slip to give the correct consistency for slip-casting.

Earthenware. Glazed pottery.

Enamel. Opaque coloured glaze.

Engobe. French term for a slip of a colour different from that of the pot's body.

Faience. Whitish pottery. Either coloured clay coated with white or glazed white clay.

Firing. The action of subjecting clay to intense heat in order to change its nature.

Frit. The basic material of glazes and enamels. A mixture of earthy and saline substances which is vitrified and crushed to form a powder.

Glaze. Transparent vitrified surface treatment.

Impasto. Italian term for partially purified coarse clay, formed by hand and fired in an open fire. Applied by archeologists to Neolithic pottery, but also denotes some popular ceramics.

Kaolin. Pure fire-clay which is one of the components of hard-paste porcelain. Called after a hill in China.

Kiln. Special oven designed for firing pottery.

Kogo. Japanese perfume box.

Koro. Japanese incense-burner.

Krater. Large-mouthed Greek or Etruscan vase used for mixing wine and water.

Lustre. Irridescent effect obtained during a third firing in a reducing atmosphere.

Lute. To cement with slip.

Mei-p'ing. Narrow-mouthed Chinese or Korean vase with a wide shoulder.

Midzu-sashi. Cold-water pot for the tea ceremony.

Ming-K'i. Chinese figures or representations of family life placed in the tombs of the dead.

Muffle-chamber. Isolated firing chamber inside the kiln, used to protect work from flame and gases.

Nicoya. Type of Central American pre-Columbian ceramics found between the gulfs of Fonseca and Nicoya.

Oinochoe. Vase for pouring wine.

Pastillage. Decoration of a pot with small balls of clay.

Petuntse. Easily melted white stone used in the composition of hard-paste porcelain.

Potsherd. Pottery fragment.

Pounce. To dust a perforated pattern sheet with coloured powder to reproduce the pattern.

Proto-porcelain. Impure dark stoneware containing kaolin used in China.

Pugmill. Machine for preparing clay for forming.

Pyxis. Box-shaped vase with a lid.

Roulette. An engraved cylinder which is rolled over wet clay to obtain a printed decoration.

Saggars. Container made of fire-clay used to isolate work during firing.

Sgraffiato. Italian word applied to a design scratched into unfired clay or engobe.

Shrinkage. The diminution in volume of a pot during firing as the water contained in the clay is burned out.

Sigillated pottery. Roman Empire ceramics with printed decoration.

Slip. A soup-like solution of clay and water.

Slip-casting. A method of reproducing original works by pouring slip into negative plaster moulds.

Stoneware. Hard opaque pottery fired at high temperatures.

Tchajins. Japanese tea masters.

Temmoku. Conical tea-bowl, generally stoneware.

Terracotta. Unglazed fired clay.

Throw. To form a pot by spinning a ball of clay centred on a wheel against the hands.

Throwing-head. The upper wheel of a double throwing-wheel on which pottery is formed.

Ushebti. Egyptian statuette with, generally, a turquoise-blue enamel, found in tombs.

Yueh. Proto-celadon from Yue-Tcheu.

SELECT BIBLIOGRAPHY

Arias and Hirmer, *Le Vase Grec*. Flammarion, 1960.

Ballardini, G., *L'Eredità ceramistica dell'antico mondo romano*. Ist. Poligrafico dello Stato, 1964.

Bellini M., and Conti, G., *Maioliche del Rinascimento*. Ed. Vallardi, 1964.

Bennett W., and Bird, J., *Andean Culture History*. American Museum of Natural History, New York, 1960.

Chewon, Kim, *Corée, 2000 ans de création artistique*. Office du Livre, Fribourg, 1966.

De Mauri, L., *L'Amatore di Maioliche et Porcellane*. Hoëpli, Milano.

Emiliani, T., *La technologia della Ceramica*. F.lli Lega, Faenza.

Fourest, H.P., *Les faïences de Delft*. P.U.F., Paris, 1957.

Giacomotti, J., *La majolique de la Renaissance*. P.U.F., Paris, 1961.

Giacomotti, J., *La céramique*. Flammarion, 1959.

Glotz, G., *La Civilisation Egéenne*. La renaissance du Livre, Paris, 1923.

Jacquemart, A., *Les merveilles de la Céramique*. Hachette, Paris, 1874.

Kidder, E., *Japon, naissance d'un Art*. Office du Livre, Fribourg, 1965.

Koechlin, A., and Migeon, G., *Art Musulman*. Ed. Massin, Paris, 1956.

Köllmann, E., *La porcelaine de Saxe*. P.U.F., Paris, 1958.

Koyama, Fujio, *Céramique ancienne de l'Asie*. Office du Livre, Fribourg, 1961.

Lee, W., *L'art de la poterie, Japon, France*. Fasquelle, Paris, 1913.

Lehmann, *Les céramiques précolombiennes*. P.U.F., Paris, 1959.

Mallowan, M.E.L., *L'aurore de la Mésopotamie et de l'Iran*. Ed. Sequoia, 1966.

Migeon, G., *Manuel d'Art Musulman*. Picard, Paris, 1927.

Noble, J.V., *The techniques of painted Attic Pottery*. Faber & Faber, London, 1966.

Pallottino, M., *Etruscologia*. Hoëpli, Milano, 1963.

Palumbo, G., Blake, H., *Ceramiche Medioevali Assisiane*. Ed. Francescana, Assisi, 1972.

Prodan, M., *La Ceramiche T'ang*. Bompiani, 1961.

Rackham, B., *Early Staffordshire pottery*. Faber & Faber, London, 1951.

Uccelli, A., *Scienza e tecnica del tempo nostro*. Hoëpli, Milano, 1958.

Dictionnaire Archéologique des techniques. Ed. de l'Accueil, Paris, 1963.

Various editions of specialist reviews: *Faenza, Bollettino del Museo Internazionale delle Ceramiche in Faenza*. Faenza (Ravenna), Italy.

Cahiers de la Céramique et des Arts du Feu. Sèvres (Seine-et-Oise), France.

Archéologie Vivante. Ed. Les publications d'Art et d'Archéologie.

TABLE OF ILLUSTRATIONS

*Illustration taken from *Les trois livres de l'Art du
Potier,* Librairie internationale, Paris, 1861.

PHOTOGRAPHIC CREDITS

Jean Arlaud, Geneva: pp. 9. 112, 115, 117, 122
Gad Borel-Boissonnas, Geneva: p. 62
Cambridge, The Fitzwilliam Museum: pp. 97
Pierre Centlivres, Berne: p. 14
Edouard Chapallaz, Duillier: p. 123
J.-P. Cottier, Geneva: cover, pp. 2, 8, 12, 13, 16 (r),
    17, 18, 19, 20, 21, 22, 23, 24, 25, 26, 27, 28, 29,
    30, 31, 36, 37, 41, 43, 44, 45, 46, 47, 50 (l), 51, 52,
    53, 54, 55, 56, 57, 77, 78, 85, 89, 91, 107, 109,
    110, 111, 114, 118, 120
Felix Eidenbenz, Zurich: p. 128
Photo Claus, Fulda: p. 124
René Funk, Geneva: p. 32
Geneva, Musée d'Ethnographie: p. 16 (l)
Geneva, Musée d'Art et d'Histoire: p. 68
Photographies et clichés Giraudon, Paris: pp. 33, 69,
    83, 101
André Held, Lausanne: pp. 61, 63, 73, 80
Photographic Archives Hirmer, Munich: pp. 6, 34,
    67, 88
Gallery Louise Leiris, Paris: p. 126
London, Victoria and Albert Museum: p. 99
London, British Museum: p. 104
Clichés des Musées Nationaux, Paris: pp. 58, 71, 74,
    79, 87
Fred Pillonel, Geneva: pp. 38, 50 (r)
Sèvres, Musée National de Céramique,
    photo R. Lalance: pp. 92, 95, 96, 103
Henri Stierlin, Geneva: p. 125
Photo Unations: p. 5
Horace van Berchem, Geneva: p. 48

The author and publishers wish to express their thanks to those who helped work on the preparation of this book; in particular Mssrs. L. Luna, G. Ermellini and Miss Z. Magnini, the directors of the *Grazia* factory, Deruta, who kindly made their workshops available for the technical photography and their staff; to Mr. Spaccini; to Mr. Mignini, curator of the Deruta Museum; to the Rev. V. Palumbo and Mr. De Giovanni, the Assisi photographer; and to all the museums and private collectors who put their documents at our disposal.
English version by Julian Snelling and Claude Namy.